"Jay Lipe is a master at taking big company marketing techniques and translating them into bite-sized chunks that small business executives can digest, and then put to immediate use."

Jim Kobs
Author of "Profitable Direct Marketing" and a member
of the Direct Marketing Hall of Fame

"Finally — an easy-to-read marketing text that both experienced and emerging entrepreneurs can understand. Whether you've been in business 20 years or 20 minutes…whether you're in technology or Tupperware®, The Marketing Toolkit for Growing Businesses *gives you immediate impact to elevate your business to the next level."*

Ron P. Wacks
President, Minnesota Homebased Entrepreneurs Association

"The Marketing Toolkit for Growing Businesses *is a key resource for any growing company marketer. And let's face it, everyone needs to market these days—from writers to self-publishers to company presidents.* The Marketing Toolkit *gives you the advice you need today to get on your marketing horse!"*

Dan Poynter
Author of "The Self-Publishing Manual"

"Jay has hit the nail on the head. The Marketing Toolkit for Growing Businesses *helps companies of all sizes plan their marketing goals and strategies. In addition, you'll find a host of useful tools to help launch your marketing initiatives."*

Jeff Prouty
CEO, The Prouty Project

"So many of today's marketing books deal with theory. But, The Marketing Toolkit for Growing Businesses *is filled with practical information that teaches you how things are actually done in the business world. It's filled with tips and tricks and will give you a running start towards developing a marketing program."*

Bob Dewar
Professor, Kellogg Graduate School of Business, Northwestern University

The
Marketing
Toolkit for
Growing
Businesses

Tips, techniques and tools
to improve your marketing

Jay B. Lipe

CHAMMERSON
PRESS

Library of Congress Control Number: 2002093302

ISBN: 0-9720345-0-1

Cover/book design by Kmf Design, Inc.

First published August 2002, by Chammerson Press, 4315 Aldrich Avenue South, Minneapolis, MN 55409-1810

NOTE: Marketing is not an overnight sensation. Anyone who decides to market a business must expect to invest a lot of time and effort in it. It is hard work.

Every effort has been made to make this book as complete and accurate as possible. However, there may be typographical and/or content mistakes. Therefore, this text should be used only as a general guide and not as the definitive source. Furthermore, this book contains information on marketing that is current only up to the printing date.

The author and publisher shall have neither liability nor responsibility to any person or entity with respect to any loss or damage caused, or alleged to have been caused, directly or indirectly, by the information contained in this book.

If you do not wish to be bound by the above, you may return this book to the publisher for a full refund.

Acknowledgements

Countless people have helped me with the preparation of this book. I am indebted to these fine people for information, feedback, and encouragement: Nancy Brenny, Hank Boubelik, Nancy Chakrin, Bob Dewar, Gayle Davis, Ph.D., Linda Furry, Beryl Deskin, Jessica Dixon, Art Dahl, Jr., Paul Esch, Rick Graw, Mark & Nancy Hostetler, Jim Kobs, Ed Kohler, John Kratz, Beth LaBreche, Tim & Kris Leary, Bob Lowe, Dan Poynter, Jeff Prouty, Norton Stillman, David Stillman, Ron P. Wacks, Warren Wechsler, Lynn Weiss and Claudia Wilson.

If I've missed someone (and I'm sure I have) I'll try to address that in Book 2! Also, I'd like to thank all of Emerge Marketing's great clients—hopefully, we taught you as much as we learned.

Very special thanks go to:
My mom Joan W. Lipe—for your incomparable editing.
My dad Jay A. Lipe—for your outstanding counsel.
My stepmom Bonnie—for demonstrating true courage.
My brother Jeff and sister Katie—for always being there.
My father and mother-in-law Dr. & Mrs. Irwin Polk—for showing how deep family love can run.
Our two kids Chandler and Carson—for teaching me what it's really all about.
My project manager on this book, Kirsten Ford—you kept us on track and on-budget. Great Job!
G.G. Ross, my grandmother—who showed me what guts it takes to strike out on your own.
Grandpa Hank and Grandma Louise, who are in Heaven now—you've got honors when we play that great course in the sky!
My wife Page—for being my best friend and the "Bin".
God—for being the lamp unto my feet.

Contents

Introduction

Is this you?

You're a manager responsible for your company's marketing, but you know way too little about it. Maybe you started in sales, or you worked your way up from the shop floor. Maybe you began in engineering, but only recently moved into marketing. Whatever the case, you're now stuck with marketing—and it's keeping you up at nights. It's not that you dislike it. What it really boils down to is that you don't understand it.

Or, is this you?

You started your company several years ago with a burning passion. Throwing pottery, developing financial plans, selling rugs, whatever it was—you were good at it.

But after the first few years went by, your clients started drying up. Word-of-mouth just didn't seem to travel as far. You had longer periods where the phone didn't ring. And every time a new wave of layoffs was announced, you saw a host of new competitors hang out their shingles.

And now you're stuck. You know you need to market your company, because without it your business will die on the vine. And if that happens you'll have to go back to working for someone else again—and you really don't want that.

Or, is this you?

You're thinking it's the right time to start your own business. You've languished long enough as someone else's employee. Now, you can step out on your own and run your business the right way.

The only thing that's holding you back though is that you've recently seen several friends' businesses go belly up, because they didn't market their companies. You've vowed that you won't make that same mistake, but what do you do next?

Or, is this you?

Your shelf is weighed down with all the marketing plans you've written.

Yet for all that time and effort, not one of them has ever been successfully implemented. They all just sit on the shelf—lifeless.

And at the end of every year, you curse yourself for plowing all that time (and many times, money) into an effort that never made it out into the market.

This one's for you

This book is written for you—all of the "you's" above. Make no mistake, today's market is *marketing driven.* Competition is international, the pace of change is dizzying and the pressures to succeed have never been greater. Those companies that have marketing plans and programs underway stand a significantly better chance of succeeding than those who just wish they were marketing.

But the real payoff to marketing is growth, long term growth, for your business. We business people focus on adding value to a company, and marketing will do that. Maybe not overnight, in a week, or even a year. But those companies that diligently commit themselves to a course of marketing, over the long haul, will add value to their bottom lines.

This book is intended to unravel the mysteries of the marketing world for you. You see, the field of marketing isn't really that complicated—it's just different from the things you already excel at. But if you read and complete the exercises in this book, and diligently commit yourself to at least a few of these principles, your marketing will be successful.

So follow along as we open up a brand new toolkit for your use—your marketing toolkit.

May your marketing emerge!

Jay B. Lipe, President, Emerge Marketing
(612) 824-4833
lipe@emergemarketing.com
www.emergemarketing.com

P.S. If you encounter questions (or answers) along the way, please don't hesitate to contact me. I'd welcome the opportunity to hear from you.

"Marketing takes
a day to learn.
But, it takes a
lifetime to master."

Philip Kotler,
Marketing guru

Chapter 1

So, What Exactly *Is* Marketing?

Let's say you just invented a brand new product—and it's perfect in every way. It performs flawlessly. It sports several new, user-friendly features. It commands a high price—and can be produced for just pennies. It's a guaranteed success, right? Wrong.

Unless the right people hear about your product, understand what it does, and know where to get it, it won't sell. That's the job of *marketing*. You see, just inventing a new product isn't enough, it's only the first step towards success. The real success comes from gaining market acceptance—and that's the job of marketing.

A pop quiz:

Which of these are marketing activities?

1. Mailing a flyer.
2. Advertising in a trade journal
3. Making a sales call on a prospect.
4. Getting interviewed on a radio station.
5. Offering a discount for a limited time.
6. Developing pricing for a new product.
7. Rolling out a new product.
8. Penetrating a new market.
9. Developing a new brochure.
10. Researching your customers.

If you said ALL, then you're right. All of these are familiar and quite common marketing activities.

Now, which of *these* are marketing activities?

1. Answering your phone.
2. Describing your business to someone at a party.
3. Interviewing job candidates.
4. Sending an email.

5. Providing an estimate.
6. Contacting an account about an overdue invoice.
7. Making your voicemail system easier to navigate.
8. Providing a referral.
9. Thanking a supplier for a job well done.
10. Returning phone calls.

Your answer? The correct answer is again, ALL of them. Surprised? Don't be. These are all points of contact between your company and its market and therefore define your company to the outside world. All happen between someone *inside* your company and someone *outside* of it, and these defining moments between your company and the outside world are the essence of marketing.

My little exercise here underscores that marketing happens, not only in the traditional senses (e.g. print advertising, brochures, direct mail), but also in your company's day-to-day interactions.

Having said this, a small business owner like you, must realize that marketing is a much wider range of activities than just promoting your business. It's not just placing ads or passing out flyers. It's not just sales. There's much, much more to it—and *everyone* in your company is a marketer.

Marketing Defined:

Marketing is a process where everyone in the company pursues actions, at designated contact points, to increase sales, grow profits and deepen relationships.

What all does marketing include?

That's all fine, you say. But exactly what makes up marketing? In 1967, Philip Kotler, a professor at Northwestern University, offered a clear definition of marketing. He saw marketing as a discipline that encompassed 4 areas—each beginning with the letter 'P'.

The 4 P's of marketing are:

Price

Place (or Distribution Channels)

Product

Promotion

Forty years later, these 4 P's still form the cornerstones of marketing. Today though, there are several more elements that have to be accounted for. They are:

People—without the right team members in place, your marketing efforts will stall.

Processes—marketing is a process, not an event. Because good marketing counts on ongoing and repetitive actions, the better your processes are developed and documented, the better your marketing will be.

Profitability—a marketer's ultimate scoreboard is the profit line. What good are sales if they don't result in a profit?

Analysis and tracking—what metrics will you use to analyze and track the progress of your marketing effort?

Now, today's small business marketing covers all these areas:

What does Marketing cover?

Price
- ○ Competitive pricing
- ○ Discounts, terms
- ○ Price/value relationship
- ○ Price elasticity

Product
- ○ Current products & services
- ○ Packaging
- ○ Value-added services
- ○ Product & service enhancements
- ○ New products & services

Place (Distribution)
- ○ Market size & coverage
- ○ Channel performance
- ○ Physical locations & their staff
- ○ Warehouse locations
- ○ Communicating with and motivating locations
- ○ Intermediaries
- ○ Communicating with and motivating intermediaries
- ○ Export & international

Promotion
- ○ Awareness
- ○ Branding
- ○ Positioning
- ○ Targeting
- ○ Key marketing messages
- ○ Marketing vehicles
- ○ Personal selling & its tools
- ○ Public image
- ○ Quality of marketing vehicles
- ○ Promotional budgets
- ○ Internal marketing
- ○ Promotional mix

People
- ○ Staff at contact points
- ○ Internal marketing staff
- ○ Marketing management staff
- ○ Sales & marketing training

Processes
- ○ Marketing planning process
- ○ Marketing checkpoint meetings
- ○ Customer feedback processes
- ○ Marketing research
- ○ Documentation of marketing processes

Analysis & Tracking
- ○ Sales analysis
- ○ Budgeting
- ○ Forecasting
- ○ Marketing expense tracking
- ○ Metrics

Profitability
- ○ Setting margins
- ○ Maintaining margins

The short of it

I'm not trying to overwhelm you here, just trying to make a point. Marketing is a broad topic that covers a lot of ground—and requires you to have a diverse toolkit.

So as you delve deeper into this book, and the world of marketing, try to keep these points in mind:

- *Everyone* markets the company, not just the marketers.
- Marketing happens at *every* contact point between your company and the outside world.
- Marketing is coordinated. All your marketing actions should be integrated with one another so as to present the clearest and most consistent impact.
- Marketing works to increase your sales *and* profits.

(The dot-com phenomenon tried to refute this by claiming marketing was a "land grab" for customers, with profits to follow later. Today, many of these dot-commers, who ascribed to this belief, no longer exist).

- In addition to sales and profits, another objective of marketing is to *deepen relationships* between a company and its audiences.
- Marketing is a process and not an event.

> *"Marketing is not a function. It is the whole business as seen from the customer's point of view."*
>
> Peter Drucker

Marketing is a process

At the risk of repeating myself, I want to reiterate that marketing is a process. And the process looks something like this:

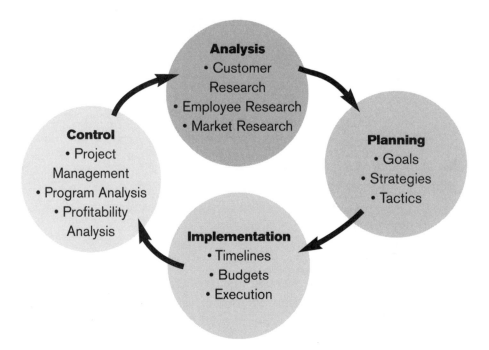

As you begin your marketing effort (or start another planning season), your first step will be to analyze your marketing situation, obtaining key marketing information along the way (Analysis).

Then, you'll feed this key information into your planning phase (Planning). Upon completing the plan, you roll it out (Implementation). And as implementation begins, so does the process of gaining feedback (Control) on your marketing efforts, which in turn, feeds back into another analysis phase, completing the cycle and starting the process over again.

If you ever get stuck in your marketing efforts, go back to this diagram. It can usually point out where you are in the process and what next steps to take to regain your momentum.

Marketing is a numbers game

You've no doubt heard this adage at a sales meeting or maybe a marketing conference. But it's all too true. Why? Because not every prospect that interacts with your company is ready to buy right then. Some might just want to have a look. Your job as marketer is to continually fill your prospect pipeline. Here's how the prospecting *pipeline* looks:

Suspects
Definition: identified consumers, either individuals or companies, who show good potential for buying a company's products or services but have not yet made contact with your company.

Prospects
Definition: identified consumers, individuals or companies, who show good potential for buying a company's products or services and have made contact with your company.

Customers
Definition: any buyer of a product or service, at any trade level.

Suspects become prospects, prospects become customers, and customers then produce referrals and positive word-of-mouth about your company which in turn, generate more suspects.

As your company's marketer, you are the owner of this prospecting process. If you're in a smaller company, you may handle all aspects of the process from uncovering new suspects, to making initial contact with them, to closing them into customers. In a bigger company, some of these duties may be performed by others (e.g. sales people). Either way, you'll want to remember that this process is the heartbeat of your company's marketing.

What it takes to succeed at marketing

1. A long-term view

We live in an instant society. We get news instantly, 24 hours a day by flicking a switch. We can prepare a meal in less than 2 minutes with a microwave. And we can buy or sell just about anything these days using a mouse and the Internet.

Given this environment, it's hard for many people to accept the notion that 99% of successful marketing happens over the long haul—weeks, months, even years. In my experience, most successful marketing efforts are borne out over time and result from:

• Patience
• Persistence
<u>and</u>
• Positive attitude.

To prove this, I'll share an experience we had with a prospect recently. The graphic below details the long and winding road our company took to convert them from a prospect into a customer:

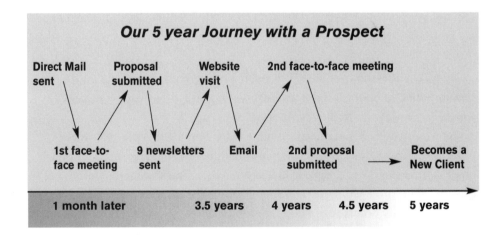

Our 5 year Journey with a Prospect

Direct Mail sent	Proposal submitted	Website visit	2nd face-to-face meeting	
1st face-to-face meeting	9 newsletters sent	Email	2nd proposal submitted	Becomes a New Client
1 month later		3.5 years	4 years	4.5 years	5 years

As you can see, it took one direct mailing, two meetings, 9 newsletters, one website visit, one email and two proposals to convert this company into a customer. And it might take *you* that long with one of yours. Are you prepared to plant marketing seeds that could take years to germinate? To succeed in marketing, you have to be in the game for the long haul.

2. Hard work

Have any of you recently started exercising? If so, you'll understand the way marketing feels when you first begin. You may procrastinate on going to the club the first time. Once at the club, you feel out of place and uncomfortable. Lifting all these weights doesn't come naturally to you and it leaves you tired. The next day, your muscles ache and you consider quitting this madness. Sound familiar? You'll feel the same way when you first start marketing your company.

Marketing is hard work. There's no easy way around it. But once you start flexing your marketing muscles, you'll be surprised at the results of your effort.

3. A love of gray

One spring day we met with a new client in the computer software industry. The discussion progressed nicely for about an hour. Then, the president looked me in the eye, took his pencil in hand and said "Okay Jay, so <u>exactly</u> how many of these software packages will we sell?" I swallowed hard.

He then continued "You know enough, by now, about this product. How many units will we ship?" I tried to explain that marketing was not a science but an art, but he didn't want to hear it. Being a trained engineer, he wanted to know *exactly* how many packages he'd sell and the formula I'd used to arrive at that number. If I couldn't tell him that, then what kind of marketer was I?

It doesn't work like that in marketing. Why? Because marketing is *gray*, it's not black and white. When you get right down to it, marketing is about changing human behavior—a customer's or a prospect's—and that just doesn't happen overnight. Marketing is an art, not a science.

4. Flexibility

Don't believe that what works for one company will automatically work for yours. If Uncle Joe's direct mail campaign produced record sales, congratulate him. But also recognize he's in another industry. Or he lives in another region of the country. Or he sells a lower priced product. Or his target audience is quite comfortable doing business through direct mail.

Based on Uncle Joe's success, you can <u>try</u> a direct mail campaign, but then be flexible enough to change directions if it doesn't achieve your objectives.

5. An innate sense of curiosity

Those with a child-like curiosity usually make the best marketers. They revel in the new. They constantly observe other company's actions and ask questions like "I wonder why Company X is doing that". They notice innovative approaches in industries far afield from their own.

With this innate sense of curiosity comes discovery. The curious marketer stumbles across a new approach that, with a little bit of tweaking, might apply to her company's marketing.

6. A sense of humility

In my 15 years of marketing, I'm sure of one thing: *You and I don't know how consumers will respond.* We may think we do, or we may have an inkling. But consumers are human beings. And because of this, they're unpredictable, emotional and (heaven forbid) influenced by other humans.

So, admit today you don't know your market, but instead, you're going to *learn* from it. Once you embrace that attitude, you'll be a far better marketer.

7. An investment attitude

Let's face it, marketing costs money. You could use this money for other purposes—like investing in your plant or equipment, or hiring additional people. But by investing in the marketing of your business, you're investing in its long-term future. Without investment in your marketing, you may never get to the point of investing in your plant or people. Think of marketing as a 401K plan for your business' health. Without investing regularly in it, you'll end up with a lot less value later on.

8. Follow through

Many marketing efforts fail because they lack adequate follow-through. Some people are just better idea-generators than implementers. Some are scared to implement because their efforts may fail. Some just aren't organized enough to visualize the many steps required.

But, what's the point of a well-conceived marketing effort if it never gets implemented? In a later chapter, I'll provide some tools to help you effectively roll out your plan, but if follow-through is your Achilles Heel, you must find a way to overcome this.

Remember...

For many business people, marketing is a black box. But it needn't be. Just view marketing as the sum total of all contacts your company has with the outside world. Accept it as a long-term process, involve everyone in your company, and you'll be headed in the right direction.

Tools To Go

- ○ <u>Everyone</u> markets the company, not just the marketers.
- ○ Marketing is coordinated. This means you must think first, then act.
- ○ Marketing occurs at <u>every</u> contact point between your company and the market. If it leaves an impression, it's marketing.
- ○ Marketing should seek to increase your sales <u>and</u> profits.
- ○ In addition to sales and profits, one goal of marketing is to *deepen relationships* between a company and its audiences.
- ○ Marketing is a <u>process</u> and not an event.

"Mistakes are the
portals of discovery."

James Joyce,
Novelist

Chapter 2

Top 12 Marketing Mistakes Growing Businesses Make

In marketing, like most things in life, success comes only after making mistakes—lots of them. I've sure made my fair share of mistakes. And I've also learned from others' mistakes in the market. So, pull up a chair and learn from our mistakes—so you don't have to make them.

I'll caution you though; this isn't an exhaustive list. With marketing so dynamic and fast-paced, new and novel marketing mistakes are made each day. But what I'll cover here are the most common marketing errors that small businesses tend to commit.

If you notice any of these things happening in your marketing, *stop* and take a step back. Each of these seemingly innocuous mistakes can be harmful, maybe even fatal, to your business.

Mistake #1 – Thinking Marketing is Advertising

"What do you do for a living?" the person standing across from me asks.

"I'm in marketing," I say.

"Oh, so you make commercials," he says.

"No, but that is a part of marketing," I reply.

"Do you sell stuff?" he asks.

"No, but that's a part of marketing too," I say.

"So what exactly do you do?" he says, a bit frustrated by now!

"As a marketer, I make sure all those things are done, PLUS I make sure we have the right products, confirm they're priced correctly, deliver them through the right channels, say the right things about them, get them in front of the right people, give those people a reason to buy, make sure they stay satisfied and then, get others to buy," I say.

"Oh!" he says (by now frantically searching the room for his next conversation).

At that point, I usually excuse myself and head for another side of the room! Yes, marketing is advertising. Yes, marketing is sales. But it's also a whole lot more.

Strategic marketing covers pricing, product matters, distribution channels, marketing communications, marketing processes and promotion (of which advertising and sales are only a part).

Achieving marketing success requires getting more from your marketing resources—time, talent, and dollars. That requires strategy—thought followed by action. Effective marketing strategies come from informed thinking, market research, and thoughtful discussion. This all supports the fact that marketing is more of a <u>process</u>. The sum total of all these actions will generate marketing success for your business.

Mistake #2 – Lacking patience

These days we expect immediate results. Want to know how your stocks are doing? Dial into the Internet for an up-to-the-minute check. Want to see what I'm looking at? I'll fax you a copy. Need to know what Kevin in Kenya, Carla in Canada and Tim in Timbuktu think? I'll set up a conference call while we're on the line.

In a world like this, is it any wonder we have short attention spans? Yet, successful marketing depends on an approach that's 180 degrees the opposite direction. Why? <u>Because marketing is about changing people's behavior.</u> And that simply doesn't happen overnight (Those of you with kids *really* know what I'm talking about!).

A while ago, I met with a fellow consultant and told him about my marketing work with growing companies. After several meetings, he assured me he'd have some business for us. Months later, after receiving my newsletter, he let me know he still had me in mind. A couple months after that, he introduced me to one of his clients—it led nowhere. Several months after that, I met with another client of his—again no deal.

A couple months go by (we're now $1^1/2$ years later and counting), and he suggested I lunch with yet another prospect of his. More meetings, lunches, and then finally, a full 2 years after meeting this gentleman, I began working with one of his clients.

Today, this company is a valued client of mine. But, what's the lesson here? *Stick it out.* If I'd given up after year one, I'd have missed out on all those revenues—and referrals.

How long should you be prepared to wait for a response to one of your ads?

Here's one thought on the subject:

The __ time a prospect sees your ad...	They...
1 st	Don't even see it.
2 nd	Don't even notice it.
3 rd	Are aware it's there.
4 th	Have a fleeting sense they've seen it somewhere before.
5 th	Actually read the ad.
6 th	Thumb their nose at it.
7 th	Get a little irritated with it.
8 th	Start to think "Here's that confounded ad again."
9 th	Start to wonder if they're missing out on something.
10 th	Ask their friends and neighbors if they've tried it.
11 th	Wonder how the company pays for all these ads.
12 th	Start to think it's a good product.
13 th	Start to feel the product has value.
14 th	Start to remember wanting a product exactly like this for a long time.
15 th	Start to yearn for it because they can't buy it.
16 th	Accept the fact that they will buy it sometime in the future.
17 th	Make a note to buy the product.
18 th	Curse their poverty for not allowing them to buy this terrific product.
19 th	Count their money very carefully.
20 th	Buy what your ad offers.

Who wrote this?
Thomas Smith, a London businessman in the nineteenth century. These words, written in 1885, still seem valid today.

It pays to be patient in marketing. According to the previous page's chart, the first three times you promote something, you're really just creating awareness. The next twelve times you're reinforcing the awareness and beginning to uncover a need. And only by the twentieth time, will your prospect take action.

Mistake #3 – Fearing failure

If you're in a small or mid-sized business, you have a key advantage over others. With your ability to take risks, you're fast and nimble and can get marketing efforts (programs, products, etc.) to market faster than others. In larger companies, marketers spend countless hours just <u>selling</u> their ideas to management (I speak from personal experience here). Not so with a small business. In a small business, you can use this time to refine and execute your ideas. You'll be in the market, while the corporate folks are still deciding if this is a good idea. Let the corporate folks waste their time with meetings, 'selling up' and face-time. By the time a big company has finally OK'd a new effort, a smaller company has tested it, refined it, and re-tested it!

All this calls for embracing *risk*, though. And you'll have to get comfortable with the notion that from time to time, you <u>will</u> fail. Remember the first time you dove off the high dive at the swimming pool? You slowly mounted the steps to the platform, and inched your way out onto the diving board. You probably chickened out a couple times (I know I did!). In the end though, you finally did it, right? And, wasn't it a kick?

We all approach new things (high dives, marketing plans, etc.) with hesitation—because we fear the worst. We envision all the bad things that might happen, without giving due consideration to the wonderful opportunities that could result. If you tend to focus on the negatives, you MUST change! Otherwise, you'll never try new things, and that spells marketing rigor mortis.

> *"From error to error, one discovers the entire truth."*
>
> Sigmund Freud, Psychologist

Several years ago, I taught classes at a well-known institution in town thinking this would generate leads from growing companies in the area. After a few semesters, I discovered instead that entrepreneurs made up the majority of students, and few growing company employees attended. So, I stopped teaching. You might consider this a marketing failure, right? It didn't achieve my objectives. I invested a lot of time, and didn't acquire any new clients.

Yet, from these classes, I discovered a whole new audience (entrepreneurs, free-lancers) for my line of Special Reports and this book. I also discovered these classes were a perfect outlet for collecting market feedback to use in writing this book.

At the end of each class, I'd throw the floor open to the class and ask questions like:

- ❍ "Which marketing programs have worked at your company?"
- ❍ "Why have they worked so well?"
- ❍ "Which marketing programs have flopped?"
- ❍ "If you could do one thing differently in your marketing, what would that have been?"

The feedback from these discussions was golden. I learned about market successes and failures. I heard first-hand, which marketing challenges were keeping them up at night. Some of this feedback reinforced what I already knew, but some of it was completely new to me.

So, was teaching these classes a failure? Absolutely not. No, it didn't produce hordes of new clients and mountains of cash, but it did provide me with key insights and knowledge. And I've come to learn, that in today's economy, *marketing knowledge is a crucial tool to have in your kit.*

Mistake #4 – Lacking diligent follow through

One client of ours was in the home-remodeling business. We had very productive discussions throughout the market planning process. He showed a good grasp of business strategies and clearly understood how these would translate into his marketing activities. But, all this momentum ground to a halt when we began implementing the marketing plan.

Suddenly, his whole demeanor changed. He endlessly nit-picked at inconsequential issues. He backed out of several marketing events. And most distressing, he couldn't meet a deadline. If he had a short section of copy to write, he'd be weeks late or never turn it in.

I quickly realized this was a fellow who liked to *create* ideas, but had a real fear of *implementing* them. This inability to get things 'out the door' means big trouble in the marketing arena. The best marketing plan in the world is useless if it sits on the shelf. How can prospects become customers if they never see anything new from you? You must commit to forward move-ment in any marketing effort—it's what turns thoughts into actions.

Regularly schedule (in your day-planner if you need to) one hour a week to work on your marketing. Write the first draft of a direct mail letter. Take a prime client out to lunch and ask her 5 basic questions about your business. Take a key source of referrals out to breakfast and ask him for 2 more. *1 hour per week is the bare minimum any company should spend on marketing.* If you're a bigger company, try spending 4 hours per week. Each of these efforts results in knowledge that fuels your marketing campaign.

Mistake #5 – Throwing nickels around like they're manhole covers

Don't get me wrong. It's very important to scrutinize where you'll spend your marketing dollars, and what payback you're expecting. But, I've seen businesses take this too far. How do you know you've gone too far?

- You catch yourself always saying "We can't afford that."
- Your vendors are too busy to work with you.
- You start hearing the word "cheap" from customers.
- Even your financial officer is urging you to spend!

Spending a bit more to improve the appearance of a marketing flyer may not result in more immediate business. Yet it does communicate a more successful image for your company. When that happens, it will pay off in sales and referrals down the road.

In marketing you must spend money. Because of this, many accountants have an inherent concern with marketers, yet spending money is necessary to get the market's attention. So, from time to time—splurge. Use an aqueous coating on your next direct mailing. Hire a graphic designer to give your materials a fresh look. Test a 2-color ad instead of 1-color.

These dollars are an investment in your marketing 'bank account'.

Mistake #6 – Resisting the use of a marketing plan

At a marketing trade show once, I surveyed close to 50 business owners. One question I asked was "Do you currently have a marketing plan?" Over 50% of them answered no. Being a devotee of marketing plans, I was astonished.

How could these companies (some of them pretty good-sized) have any confidence in their marketing without a plan? It would be like driving cross-country without a map. Sure, you'd probably get to your final destination, but think of all the detours and dead-ends you'd encounter!

A marketing plan forces you to think ahead and visualize strategic issues for your business like:

○ What business are we in?
○ Who are our best customers?
○ What benefits do our products/services provide to customers?
○ What are our business strengths? What do our customers rave about?
○ Where will future business come from?

When you commit your answers to paper, something profound happens. Suddenly you see quite clearly why you're in business, where you're headed, what makes your company special and why marketing program "A" makes sense while program "B" doesn't.

We'll talk more about the specific steps involved in developing your marketing plan in later chapters. But whether you use my market planning process, yours, or someone else's, use somebody's! *Developing a marketing plan creates the foundation for a successful marketing effort.*

Mistake #7 – View marketing as a miracle cure

To my constant surprise (and chagrin), many folks view marketing as the magic answer to their ills. They set off down the marketing road, but just short weeks later—without a 'home run' to their credit—get discouraged and quit the effort.

Seeking an immediate turnaround to their business fortunes, these folks place one ad and then envision a madhouse of activity as their phones are swamped with callers. Folks, it doesn't happen that way.

Do you know how high the first Mercury Space Rocket flew? 4 *inches*! Immediately after ignition, an engine malfunctioned and the onboard computers shut the engines down, while the rocket descended—a grand total of four inches—back to earth. Did the space program throw in the towel? No. After several more successful (and a few failed) missions, the Mercury program transformed into the Apollo program, which eventually landed humans on the moon—ranking as one of mankind's ultimate achievements.

> *"Only those who dare to fail greatly can ever achieve greatly."*
>
> Robert F. Kennedy

In most cases, marketing won't save a company. It will only *start* saving it. As I mentioned earlier, two keys to successful marketing are patience and persistence. This means you may have to wait a while for the full impact of your marketing.

Mistake #8 – Putting all your eggs in one marketing basket

We've all met one-dimensional people, haven't we? They talk on and on about only one thing. The result? Boring! This is a little like the company that markets only one way to its prospects. What happens? The prospects get bored. Don't let this happen to you.

Instead, seek *variety* in your marketing attempts. Variety keeps prospects on their toes—wondering what you'll do next. Variety also keeps you front and center in a prospect's mind. By seeing your company in a variety of ways, they'll more easily remember you.

When someone says to me "I've seen your name a lot recently, but I can't remember where," I take this as a compliment. It means we've marketed using a variety of tools, and kept the audience a little off balance.

Variety also helps you get picked up on others' radar screens. A media editor may single you out as an expert after hearing you speak to an audience. A vendor in your industry, after receiving your direct mail piece, may contact you with a referral. A contact in a different industry may tell prospects about you after reading a trade magazine article about your business.

Think of marketing as so many drops of water in a bucket. You may never know which drop overturns the bucket, but each drop does its part.

Mistake #9 — Do it all in-house

Let's face it, when you first start out in business you'll do most of your own marketing. You'll write press releases, design your brochures and even lick the stamps for your direct mail. But over time, your business will grow to where you can't do it all anymore. At this point, you'll have to turn to outsiders and in my opinion, very good things come from this.

Whether it's outside graphic designers, copywriters, marketing consultants or others, outsiders bring several advantages to your business:

• Extra arms and legs

Outsiders help you accomplish more. With their help, you'll launch more programs and complete more projects. As a result, you'll stay in front of your prospects more often.

• A view of the forest

Some clients we work with hire us because they're too close to the action to see the bigger marketing picture. Or as one of my associates says "They're too busy looking at the bark, to even see the forest." Because they're so caught up in the daily grind of their business, they need someone who can help them take stock of the big picture. A good outside marketer will keep you focused on the important issues, not just the urgent ones.

• A few new lessons

Whenever I bring in an outside marketer to work on our business, I usually end up learning far more than I expect to. A good outside marketer stretches your thinking and just might provide a brand new idea or way of thinking.

These people can stretch you on the little things, like your website's format or the color of your logo. Or they'll stretch you on big things, like creating your business mission or targeting a potential market.

But each outsider brings a wealth of marketing experience to your door. This knowledge represents the sum total of their marketing experiences and you will be the better for tapping into it.

Mistake #10 — Say something today, something different tomorrow

These days, it's estimated each person views over 3,000 marketing messages *per day*. This means your marketing messages will compete with 2,999 other messages that day. So, all your marketing messages should be crystal clear. People just aren't listening with 100% attention these days. And, if your messages (including copy, visuals, brand identity and positioning) lack consistency, you're making the prospect work too hard.

Use consistent imagery and messages throughout all your marketing. That way, when prospects are exposed to your marketing efforts, they know it's from you and noone else.

One client of ours is a first-ring suburb of Minneapolis. After reviewing that city's signage (road signs, park signs, vehicle stickers, etc.), we noticed a lack of consistency. Old logos appeared on some signs, while an updated logo was featured on others. Moreover, many police cars and uniforms didn't display any city logo. As a result, when the city police showed up at a resident's house, some residents weren't sure if those cars and officers were really from their suburb! The result was a confusing and inconsistent image for the city as seen through the eyes of its residents.

Mistake #11 – Fail to emphasize face-to-face marketing

If I told you a business' marketing consisted of only these elements:

- Direct Mail
- Billboards
- Internet
- Print Advertising

would you be impressed...or concerned? I'd be concerned. Why? Because all of these marketing efforts are *non-personal*. They don't involve face-to-face contact between a prospect and the business. That's bad.

These days we're bombarded with ads on television, ads on websites, ads on the radio, ads in the newspaper, ads on buses, ads on cars, ads along the side of the road. Ads, ads, ads. Shoot, we even have ads in our bathrooms, and I hear ads are now appearing *inside* the urinals!

What do people look for these days? People they can trust. Therefore, your marketing should strive to "show the company face" to your prospects. Be human. Be personal. Be a face.

If you or your company does any of the following, you're pursuing personal marketing:

- ○ Personal Selling
- ○ Trade Shows
- ○ Networking
- ○ Open Houses
- ○ Demonstrations
- ○ Seminars
- ○ Workshops
- ○ Speaking Engagements
- ○ Presentations

If you're leaving these out of your marketing toolkit you're shortchanging your effort. Give prospects a chance to see the face of your company. If you don't, they'll never know its personality!

Mistake #12 – Closing your ears to the market

Marketing is about being "in the market". A crucial part of that is keeping your ears open. Large companies have the resources to conduct massive market research programs. Yet, many small business owners wrongly assume they can't afford research.

I'd argue two things. First, ongoing market research should be a mandatory part of any small business. And second, all small businesses can afford market research if they just view it creatively.

Each of these is a market research question:

- ○ What are we doing well?
- ○ What could we improve?
- ○ What more can we do for you?

If you ask these questions to three of your customers every quarter, and then listen hard to the answers, you're doing research.

Remember...

None of us can avoid all these marketing mistakes. Sometimes, I find myself slipping back into some of them in our marketing business. But just knowing what they are and keeping a watchful eye out for them makes you a better marketer.

Tools To Go

Work to avoid these common marketing mistakes:

○ Thinking marketing is advertising.
○ Lacking patience.
○ Fearing failure.
○ Lacking diligent follow through.
○ Throwing nickels around like they're manhole covers.
○ Resisting the use of a marketing plan.
○ Viewing marketing as a miracle cure.
○ Putting all your marketing eggs in one basket.
○ Doing it all in-house.
○ Saying something one day, something different the next.
○ Failing to emphasize face-to-face marketing.
○ Closing your ears to the market.

Review this list every 6 months.

"From now on the key is knowledge. The world is becoming not labor intensive, not materials intensive, not energy intensive, but knowledge intensive."

Peter Drucker,
Author

Chapter 3

Getting The 4-1-1: How To Assess Your Company's Marketing

Back in the 1980's, I was Marketing Manager for a consumer products company and reported to a boss who was a solid strategic thinker. During the holiday break however, he was seriously injured in an accident and would be absent from the office for months. In short, I was on my own.

A week after his accident, I got a call from the Food & Drug Administration informing me that one of our products, a specialty cereal, was going to be recalled. After some quick calculations, I realized a nationwide recall would cost this company millions of dollars, not to mention the irreparable harm it would cause the product's reputation.

As I talked to my boss in the hospital, his words of wisdom still ring in my ears today. He said "Jay, don't neglect the information-gathering stage." With his advice as a guiding light, I decided to dig deeper, get more opinions, and find out everything I possibly could about this particular type of recall before I accepted the FDA's word on the matter.

Over the next month, I spoke with sales reps, distributors, representatives from the overseas manufacturer, lab workers, members of the FDA and scores of other contacts. I had our in-house research and development staff test and retest the cereal to determine if the FDA was correct. In short, I promised myself I'd accept the Administration's recommendation only after I'd proved it to myself.

A month later we presented our findings to the FDA, fully refuting their claim. And largely because we presented a great deal of well-researched information, the FDA overturned its recall recommendation.

If there's a lesson for you it's this: Good information is a crucial marketing tool. If you put serious time and effort into gathering the right information for your marketing plan, your subsequent efforts will pay off in spades.

Your first step – inside the four walls

It stands to reason that before you can address your marketing problems, you must first know what they are. Your first step then is to conduct an internal assessment to help uncover your marketing problems.

During the marketing assessment, your objective is simple—collect knowledge. You have to be diligent, inquisitive, and above all else, ready to accept the unvarnished truth. Some of it you'll love. To hear one of your customers wax on about how important your company is to their success can be downright intoxicating.

But plan also on hearing the *REAL* reason you lost your biggest account, or the truth behind why you're losing employees to your competitor. That's okay. This knowledge, as painful as it is to hear, proves invaluable when you reach the marketing plan stage.

The more closely you listen at this stage, the more your marketing will benefit down the road.

The two views

There are two ways to view your business: *internally* (or inside the maze as I like to think of it) and *externally* (kinda like 3 stories above the maze). The *internal view* looks at your business through the eyes of those inside it. This includes staff employees, field employees, board members, advisory board members. It could even include ex-employees, retired employees or outside consultants currently working with your business. These people are familiar with your business' personality and are best suited to comment on its strengths and weaknesses.

The *external view* sees your business through the eyes of outsiders. These might be customers, suppliers, analysts, the media, even employee spouses. All these folks view your company through a different set of lenses and, as a consequence, see a different side of your company.

A good, thorough marketing assessment gathers information from both viewpoints. This is especially important when seeking the complete picture because information from one view can serve to crosscheck the other. I'll give you an example.

A client of ours in the commercial travel business had very definite opinions about what made it unique to its customers. Yet, when I interviewed 5 of their biggest customers, I learned otherwise.

Our client believed the ultimate benefit it provided to its customers was significant savings in the form of lower priced airline tickets. Yet when I spoke with our client's customers, they focused on another, more unique benefit. These customers placed a much higher value on the client's proactive, travel management services (e.g. management reporting and benchmarking, travel & entertainment expense management, travel policy development & implementation).

When the client heard its customers waxing on about its travel management abilities, suddenly the client saw a brand new opportunity open up for them. As a result of this valuable customer feedback, our client decided to reposition itself.

When was all said and done, the client underwent a rebranding effort that produced an updated company name, logo, tagline and key marketing messages. The result was a much stronger (and sharper) company image.

Some key reports

As a first step, you'll generate some standard marketing and sales reports. What you're looking for in these reports are clues to the overall marketing health of your business. Some reports you may already use, others you may only look at occasionally, and still others you haven't generated yet.

But by pulling together these reports, you'll peel away the first layer of your analysis. The first reports you need include:

- **Overall sales report**

This one helps assess your sales situation, year-over-year. How have your total sales been across the past three years? Are they trending up or down? Your report should look something like this:

	2002	% (+/-)	2001	% (+/-)	2000
Total Sales	$12,760,000	+24%	$10,300,000	+4%	$9,928,000

- **Overall profit & loss statements (P&L's)**

At the same time you look at sales, you should look at profitability. This report should look like this:

	2002	**% (+/-)**	**2001**	**% (+/-)**	**2000**
Gross Profits	$2,020,000	-3%	$ 2,080,000	+4%	$ 1,995,000
Net Profits	$1,100,000	-11%	$ 1,235,000	+4%	$1,185,000

Note that in this report, we're measuring two different levels of profitability:

1. Gross Profits

(the difference between sales and your cost of goods/services sold) <u>and</u>

2. Net Profits

(gross profits with all marketing & sales expenses backed out).

Over a three-year horizon, do these profit figures trend the same way as sales? On page 39, you'll see that the company's sales jumped 24% from 2001 to 2002, yet the gross profit (above) dropped -3%, and the net profit fell even further –11%. As a marketer, this situation signals that expenses are growing faster than sales and additional sales are coming at the expense of profitability.

- **Profitability by customer (or product)**

The next report helps you "peel away another layer of the onion" by examining the profitability of your individual customers or products.

If you're a consumer products company with several different products, it will be instructive to analyze individual products for profitability. For business-to-business companies, it may be more helpful to look at profitability by customer (or even by project). Here's how to do that:

Profitability By Customer

<u>Start with</u> all Customer Revenue	$2,400,000
<u>Subtract Total Costs</u> of this Customer	− $600,000
• Cost of goods sold	
• Staff dedicated to this customer	
• Overhead expenses	
<u>Equals</u> total Customer Profit	$1,800,000
<u>Divided by</u> total Customer Revenue	÷ $2,400,000
<u>Equals</u> Margin %	75%

If you do this for several of your customers (or products) you can then compare them. Then, ask yourself these questions:
- Which customers are more profitable? Why?
- What makes some customers less profitable?
- Knowing these margins now, would you continue working with all these customers?

If you're a larger company, a good cost accounting system makes this job easier. But even if your aren't, you can still get to this metric using broad assumptions, a sharp pencil and a calculator.

• New product sales

When I worked for a large consumer goods company, we tracked new product revenue (they considered 'new products' to be anything launched within the last 5 years) religiously. This is an important marketing barometer because buyers these days are accustomed to new products. In fact in 2000 alone, consumer goods companies churned out more than 31,000 new products! Whether or not we need this many new products is beside the point. We marketers have created a market that expects a steady stream of new products, and so we must market in that environment.

Generate a report at each year-end that identifies your sales by new product revenue (products or services that have been launched within 5 years) and old product revenue. As a rule of thumb, 10-15% of your revenues each year, should come from new products or services.

• New customer sales

Customers go away for a variety of reasons. They may switch to your competitors, take the business in-house, or they may even go out of business. You have to plan on this attrition—it's a fact of business. To supplant this, you must find a steady stream of new customers, and tracking your new customer efforts is a good first step.

To start, let's define a new customer as any company (or consumer) with *12 months or less* sales history with you. As each new year begins, compile a report listing all new customers ranked by sales. This should look like this:

Customer	Annual Sales	Source (how did they come to you?)
Jayskee, Inc.	$1,300,000	Referral–Fred Smith
Anderson Corp.	753,000	Website
Jones, Inc.	562,000	Referral–Mayer Printing
Applegate Inc.	354,000	Direct Mail

• New leads

Leads act as the fuel for the marketing operations of a business. A lead is someone who has signaled interest in developing a relationship with your company. They could have:
- Called for a brochure.
- Left you a card at a trade show.
- E-mailed you, asking a question.
- Sent in a reply card.
- Registered on your website.
- And countless others…

When someone approaches your company and initiates a dialogue, it means you've piqued their interest. And the more leads your company generates, the more business you'll get.

Track your leads on a *monthly* basis. Any less often and you won't have adequate time to react to market developments. We use a form like this to track leads for our company:

Emerge Marketing   Lead Tracking Form
Year_____

Name	Company	Source	Inquiry Date	Proposal Date	Project Go-ahead Date
Bill Dexter	Ramsey Assoc	Referral-Joe Babcock	4/02	6/02	8/02

- **Best customer report**

Which customers contribute the most to your overall sales? Do they continue to buy from you in increasing amounts? How did they come to your company? Compile a report that ranks your customers, by sales, for the previous year. The top 10 on this list will be the companies or customers that are the backbone of your company. Once you've identified them, you can actively target them with campaigns to boost their sales or generate referrals.

- **Sales & marketing expense analysis**

The last report you'll need is one that tracks your marketing & sales spending by category. If you're searching for which categories to track, here are some basic ones that might be helpful:

	This Year	**Last Year**	**% +/-**
Advertising	$	$	
Brochures/flyers			
Coop marketing programs			
Direct Mail programs			
Directories			
Email programs			
Identity work (logo, etc)			
Packaging			
Point-of-Purchase materials			
Postage			
Premiums			
Presentations			
Promotions			
Publicity			
Research			
Sales kits			
Selling Materials			
Signage			
Telemarketing			
Trade Shows			
Uniforms			
Yellow Pages			
Website			
Marketing Personnel			
Sales Personnel			
Travel & entertainment			
Other			

What do you notice here? Which of these expense categories are highest? Are your expenses for certain categories growing faster than your sales? Going forward, are you still comfortable spending at these levels?

A final note on reports

You do <u>not</u> have to use all these reports. Just pick and choose those that make sense for your business. Using just a few of these, you'll be amazed at how quickly you can sniff out opportunities and problems in your marketing.

But let me caution you about one thing. Don't spend too much time here. Too many companies I know start into this analysis phase yet months later, are still generating and analyzing reports.

The trick in this phase is to *keep moving*. Develop a few of these reports, analyze them, arrive at some conclusions—and then move on. You've got more ground to cover.

The next step; Interviewing those inside your walls

After compiling and analyzing the reports, you can now turn your attention to information gathering with internal sources. Among the most valuable to interview are:

- Marketing staff
- Sales representatives
- Telemarketers
- Complaint handlers
- Delivery personnel
- Customer service employees
- Repair staff
- Purchasing staff
- Anyone who deals directly with customers, including receptionists and administrative staff.

In short, you want to bend everyone's ear that has contact with the customer. Since these people talk daily with your customers, they are a valuable resource for key insights.

Oftentimes these people can provide valuable insights into your company's image, products, services, staff, because they see them from your customer's eyes. And because they'll speak with these same customers again tomorrow, and likely hear the same complaints as yesterday, they have a vested interest in voicing their opinions to you. You see, if any marketing solution you put together addresses their complaints, then it will make their jobs easier.

What to ask these internal sources

One thing I've learned in internal assessments is to make sure you ask *the same questions* of every person you interview. That way, when you consistently hear the same answer to a certain question—from all types of employees—you'll know you've uncovered a problem. So, if you hear from entirely different departments that the Holiday Promotion was much more trouble than the sales it brought in (even though you came up with the concept), you'll know this issue must be addressed.

Here are some basic questions you can ask all interviewees:

1. What are our strengths?

_____

_____

_____

_____

2. What do our customers rave about?

_____

_____

_____

_____

3. What are our weaknesses?

_____

_____

_____

_____

4. What do our customers complain about most?

_____

_____

_____

_____

5. What are our greatest opportunities?

_____

_____

_____

_____

6. What are our greatest threats?

_____

_____

_____

_____

Note that questions 1-4 help identify issues within your *internal* environment, while questions 5 & 6 help you flesh out your company's *external* issues.

As you collect this data, I recommend creating a standard form with these 6 questions and space for each answer. Then, after collecting and recording each interviewee's responses on a separate form, you can compare the forms and see the overlaps. Those answers that repeatedly come back (e.g. "Nobody knows who we are in our market", "Our competitors outspend us in marketing" or "The aging baby boomers present a great product opportunity for this company") signal a consensus on the real issues. When you identify the most common issues in each category, I recommend entering them into a SWOT (Strengths, Weaknesses, Opportunities & Threats) Grid like the one below:

Example–SWOT Grid	
Strengths	**Weaknesses**
• Innovative products • Outstanding customer service • We offer on-line purchasing	• Prices are too high vs. competitor XYZ • Packaging isn't sturdy • Little name awareness
Opportunities	**Threats**
• Our website could be updated to add a fresher image • Drop-shipping would save us inventory costs	• Imports from Far East • Competitor opening a store 3 blocks away • Dot-com competitors without retail stores who offer lower prices

After finishing the grid, you'll wind up with an at-a-glance summary of key issues as seen from inside your company's four walls.

Remember...

In this phase of your marketing, you're charting a course for discovery. As you sail the seas of data and opinion, don't be surprised if you encounter some choppy water. But, using open ears and a probing mind as your compass and sextant, you'll very likely find the best route to your destination.

Tools To Go

○ Don't neglect the information gathering stage.

○ Seek a well-balanced assessment by collecting internal *and* external feedback.

○ Generate several of these reports and use them to identify issues:

1. Overall Sales Report

2. Overall Profit and Loss Report

3. Profitability by Customer (or Product)

4. New Product Sales

5. New Customer Sales

6. New Leads

7. Best Customer Report

8. Sales & Marketing Expenses

○ Seek out internal interviews with people who serve your customers.

○ Fill out a SWOT form with the most recurring issues you uncover.

"It's not what you don't know that will hurt you. It's what you think you know that just ain't so."

Satchel Paige,
Baseball player

Chapter 4

Outside The Four Walls: Researching Your Market for Valuable Information

Getting an internal view of your company through reports and employee interviews is one thing. But for a truly balanced view of your marketing, you'll want the opinion of your market.

I've seen businesses assume one thing (i.e. "Our prices are in-line with the competition", "People love our products", "We don't have any competition") only to learn an entirely different story from their market. Folks, marketing is about *tapping into your market* and outside research is one primary tool for doing this.

The 5 basic steps in a business research program

Step 1 – Customer 1-on-1's

Your first stop in gathering external information is your customers. They literally have a relationship with your company and, as a result, can supply you with intimate details about its strengths and weaknesses. Your first task then is to speak, face-to-face, with 5 customers. If at all possible when selecting these five, try to make them a mix of the following:

• Current, satisfied customers
• New customers (with less than 1 year of sales history)
• Lapsed customers (those who were once customers, yet now haven't ordered for a year or more) <u>and</u>
• Prospects.

You'll ask the same questions to each, but be prepared to get answers that are quite different. Each conversation should last between 30-60 minutes and ideally, should be held at a neutral location (i.e. a coffee bar or over lunch).

Try to get them away from their offices or homes so you have their undivided attention, and they, in turn, provide thoughtful answers to your questions. Use some or all of the questions below, but feel free to probe deeper if you feel you're onto something.

Customer 1-on-1 Questions

Background Questions

1. How long have you been a customer of (your company)?

_____

_____

_____

2. How did you first learn about (your company)?

_____

_____

_____

3. At that time, why did you become a customer of (your company)?

_____

_____

_____

Current Purchasing Environment

4. With respect to (your industry) what are the biggest challenges you face?

_____

_____

_____

5. How does (your company) help you with these challenges?

_____

_____

_____

Competitive Environment

6. Who are (your company's) biggest competitors? What are their strengths & weaknesses?

Competitor	Strengths	Weaknesses

Your Company's Profile

7. What are (your company's) greatest strengths? Weaknesses?

Strengths	Weaknesses

8. What does (your company) do, that noone else does in the market?

_____

_____

_____

9. What would it take for you to stay with (your company) for 5 years?

_____

_____

_____

New Products & Services

10. What other capabilities or services would you like to see (your company) offer?

_____

_____

_____

Marketing & Sales

11. How often do you hear from (your company)?

_____

_____

_____

12. What methods do they use to keep in touch with you?

_____

_____

_____

13. Which of (your company's) competitors does the best job of marketing? How do they market their company?

_____

_____

_____

14. Anything else you'd like to add?

_____

_____

_____

Step 2 – Interviews with influencers

After you've talked with your customers, now pursue conversations with one or two *influencers* for your business. These are outsiders who know your business well, but from a non-customer perspective. They could be:

○ Board members
○ Media editors or reporters
○ Trade association executives
○ Consultants
○ Your company's bankers, accountants, or lawyers

Ask them the same questions you've asked your customers and see if their answers differ.

An outsider might help here

For these first two steps, if you can afford it, consider hiring an outsider—either a consultant or researcher—to conduct the interviews. Why? Because most customers won't be entirely open with you. They may hold back their opinions for fear of damaging your relationship or hurting your feelings.

I've interviewed numerous of my clients' customers and conducted many research projects and I've always managed to glean key information that my client could not. I feel this is mainly because I (as a consultant) am considered to be an objective, third-party. Because I'm an outsider, these people feel more comfortable telling me the unvarnished truth, and that is critical information that can then be funneled back into our client's marketing process.

Step 3 – Identify your touchpoints

The next step now is to identify your company's *touchpoints*. Think of a touchpoint as any point of contact between your business and the marketplace. These fall into two categories—customer and prospect touchpoints.

Customer touchpoints include:

- O Voicemail
- O Extranet sites
- O Emails from your company
- O Faxes
- O Phone receptionists
- O Product shipments
- O Company invoices
- O In-store kiosks & terminals
- O Credit & collections departments
- O Help lines
- O Customer service

First, identify all touchpoints that connect your company with its customers. Then, list them on a form like the one on the next page.

Next, rank them in terms of importance using the priority ranking values indicated in the box. Then, for those touchpoints ranked "3", identify some weaknesses and actions steps you can take to address them.

In the example already entered in the form, I've identified voicemail as a critical touchpoint for this company (and it is for many companies). Then I've listed several weaknesses and come up with a few ideas to address them.

Remember that each touchpoint can be an opportunity for two-way communications with your market. What is said at each touchpoint, and how it's said, leaves a lasting impression about your company.

Touchpoint	Priority	Weaknesses	Ways to Improve it...
Voicemail	3	Too long; too many options; not marketing oriented	• Trim options • Mention website

Priority Rankings

3 – Critical: Must address in < 6 mos.

2 – Important: Must address in < 1 Yr.

1 – Issue: Can address in > 1 Yr.

Prospect touchpoints **are communication points between your company and prospects, and as such involve more selling and persuading.**

These include:
- ○ Direct mail
- ○ Visiting your website
- ○ Word-of-mouth mentions
- ○ Advertisements
- ○ Reading an article on your company
- ○ Brochures

- ○ Networking at a convention
- ○ Sales calls
- ○ Presentations
- ○ Estimates & proposals
- ○ Contracts
- ○ Hearing you speak at a seminar
- ○ Trade show booths

These are only a few, but just like customer touchpoints, each prospect touchpoint must leave people with a high degree of confidence in doing business with your company.

Step 4 – Customer satisfaction surveys

To keep the lines of communication open with your customers, you might want to consider using a customer satisfaction survey. These surveys help you keep tabs on how well you're doing with your customers, but they can also help head off potential problems.

Given everyone's preoccupation with time, we keep our company's survey to one page. It's a fax-back survey with just 5 questions, and we've received back 90% of all surveys.

Here are some questions that are commonly used in a survey like this:

○ What one thing did you like about doing business with us?
○ What one thing would you change?
○ When you bought our product, what did you really end up with?
○ On a scale of 1 to 10, please rate us on the job we did for you.
○ What will it take for you to stay with us for 5 years?

One of our clients, a specialty paper manufacturer, uses an annual customer satisfaction survey to measure their progress against its competitors. They ask their customers to rate them, and their competitors, on 10 different aspects of their products and service. When they receive the survey results, they then know the key weaknesses they must address in the following year. Every year they then repeat the survey and measure how well they've improved against their previous year's results.

Step 5 – Competitive intelligence

Do you have an ongoing competitive surveillance program? Don't worry, most growing businesses don't. Yet, so much of what your competitors do impacts your marketing, doesn't it? If your competitor launches a new product, won't that impact the products you offer? If your competitor's brochure targets a new type of customer, couldn't this affect your targeting? If you don't have a competitive surveillance program—start one today.

Simply label a folder "Competition" and place it in a file drawer that's accessible to all in your company. Then, establish a goal of obtaining information about your top five competitors. And I'd recommend involving other company employees in this effort. For example, as you recruit other staff members to assist you, make them the "chief sleuth" for one of your competitors.

Most competitive information can be found in the public domain. Some of the most common sources of competitive information include:

- Competitors' web sites
- Annual reports
- Brochures obtained at trade shows
- Articles appearing in trade publications
- Advertisements
- Yellow page ads
- Local want ads
- CD-ROM databases such as Dun & Bradstreet's *Million Dollar Directory*.
- Directories like *The Corporate Directory*, which lists over 9500 firms in the US and includes data such as SIC code, number of employees, sales history and the basics of ownership

Once you've obtained the competitive information, share it with all employees who regularly interact with customers and prospects. You'll probably also want to review it with members of your executive staff or your marketing team. As you review the information, ask these questions:

❍ Are *they* doing something we should be doing (e.g. targeting a market, selling a product, bundling a service, pricing differently, selling into another channel)?

○ What are we doing that they aren't?

○ What actions should we take to respond to what they're doing?

As you add to this competitive file, carve out time to review the file with the appropriate staff every 6 months. Some may not have seen the latest information, while others might have missed looking at the file altogether.

Your competitive intelligence effort is sure to generate a raft of opportunities and learning. Stick with this intelligence gathering process and you'll be surprised how it drives marketing improvements within your company.

Some other types of research

Lapsed customer surveys

Another survey approach my company has used with success is the lapsed customer survey. Mailed to people or companies, who were once customers yet haven't purchased from you in the last two years, this survey can actually reactivate dormant accounts. In fact, one lapsed customer survey we developed for an industrial services firm resulted in over $700,000 in sales!

Always remember that the primary objective of this survey is to gather information about their purchase experience with you. However, after you've probed for the reasons they left, you have every right to ask questions like:

• "Would you be interested in having a rep from our company contact you?" or

• "Are there any other individuals or companies you know who might benefit from our services?"

Mystery shopping

Used widely by the retail industry, these studies hire an outsider to pose as a customer shopping at your company's store. These studies will help you identify strengths and weaknesses in the following areas:

• Store appearance

• Service quality

• Selling skills of your personnel

• Product selection

• Pricing

To get the best results for this type of research, hire an outside firm and be very specific about the kind of feedback you're seeking.

Customer Clubs

When I was marketing director at a mattress manufacturer, every three months we'd host an informal conversation with our customers. We'd invite 5-10 customers to our company headquarters, and conduct a no-holds-barred conversation about our products and marketing methods. Boy, were they flattered!

Over popcorn and soft drinks, we'd show them new product prototypes or share preliminary ad concepts. We might even show them proofs of new marketing materials we were developing. All of this proved extremely valuable in developing our product mix and marketing messages.

Just as important, these customers left the meetings with a renewed feeling of loyalty. We'd cared enough to ask for their input, and most were very appreciative of that fact. I'd highly recommend customer clubs as a valuable way to seek input and tighten relationships, no matter your business.

Some other dirt-cheap research methods

Real-time web research

More and more companies are attaching real-time research questionnaires on their websites. You can capture great feedback and generate repeat traffic as the respondents check back on the results. Check out www.web-survey.net, www.powerfeedback.com, or www.surveymonkey.com.

Call your switchboard and ask for yourself

This can be an eye-opener. How well does your receptionist answer the phone? Does she represent the brand well? Ask her what your company does. How does she answer? Now, ask for your customer service department. How long does it take to transfer you? Do you encounter a cheerful on-hold messaging system or is the silence deafening? When you finally connect with the customer service department, does it live up to its name? This is research from your customers' point of view.

Read Your Customer Mail

If customers mail you letters, spend an hour each month reading some of them. If you're looking for the unvarnished truth, you're sure to find it here.

One final thing before launching any survey

Whatever survey method you choose, <u>always</u> pre-test it. A *pre-test* is where you test the survey, with one or two people, before rolling it out to a much larger audience.

I suggest you pre-test your survey with these people in person, because this allows you to read their body language. Are they confused by this question? Why? Would another question make better sense?

This pre-testing step ensures you get the final kinks out of the survey before launching it to a much wider audience. We recently developed a survey for apartment property managers. Before sending it out though, we ran it by a local property manager for her input. The results were startling. She misunderstood several questions that we then reworded, and actually suggested other questions to ask. The result was a vastly improved survey.

Who should you pre-test the survey on? Possible options are:
- Peers in your industry
- Fellow employees
- Customers you're very familiar with
- College professors <u>and</u>
- Spouses

After pre-testing the survey, make any required changes to the survey and you're ready to field it.

How many people do you need to survey?

Most of the survey methods I've described above won't produce statistically significant results. That's because you would have to sample close to 400 people to produce a statistically significant survey. But don't let this discourage you. I've gotten very helpful survey results from talking with only five people. If you have a large number of customers, and can't afford to get 400 respondents, try to obtain 40-50. If you have a much smaller customer base (i.e. clients in a smaller business) try to get 10 responses. Whatever response you get though, I guarantee you'll come away with valuable and actionable feedback.

Remember...

Many companies see market research as a one-time activity—send out one survey, read the results, then move on. I view marketing research as an *ongoing marketing strategy*. It can determine customer satisfaction, provide feedback on weaknesses the company must address, identify competitive threats, uncover new markets, or even identify prospects. Do you know of any other marketing vehicle, aside from live sales people, that can do this much? To me, marketing research is so important to a growing business that it should form a cornerstone of your marketing effort.

Tools To Go

○ If at all possible, conduct face-to-face interviews with customers and influencers. Hire someone to do this if you can.

○ Identify your customer and prospect touchpoints. Then, identify action steps to improve those with the highest priority.

○ Regularly survey your customers. You'll not only get valuable feedback but they'll be glad you asked.

○ Always pre-test a survey as a way to "debug" it before "going live".

"Plans are nothing;
planning is everything."

Dwight D. Eisenhower,
Military General &
U.S. President

Chapter 5

6 Reasons Every Company Needs a Marketing Plan

So now that you've finished the analysis stage, do you just throw some programs out there on the street? No. All too often, I see businesses move directly from the analysis stage to the implementation stage without doing any *planning*. And the dialogue goes something like this:

"Hey Joe, I was talking with Bill at Zippidee Company (one of their biggest customers), and he said he stopped by Barebones Inc.'s (one of their biggest competitors) booth at the Hodown Annual Trade Show," the sales manager says to the president.

"Zippidee was at the Hodown?" answers the president, "Well then, we gotta be at that trade show next year. Sue, call the trade association and reserve a booth for next year's show. Al, get some information about the show. Sally, start recruiting reps to work the booth. Jim, reorder the beer mugs with our logo from the premium supplier—we'll hand those out at the booth. Come on people, let's moooooooove."

Is this proper marketing? Of course not. This scenario demonstrates how, all too often, a company can begin implementing tactics without first thinking strategically. It's a lot like cooking without a recipe. Toss in a little of this, try a dash of that and stir until you think it's done. That may work for experienced cooks like my grandmother, but it doesn't work well for marketing. After all, I had to eat my grandmother's cooking mistakes (*"Three bites Jay, then you can go play with your army soldiers"*)—but the market doesn't have to accept yours!

All good marketing begins with a marketing plan

The cornerstone of any successful marketing effort is the marketing plan. Why? Here are six reasons why a marketing plan should act as the foundation for your marketing effort:

#1 – A marketing plan lays the groundwork for action

Nothing is more forceful than committing your ideas to paper. If you say to yourself "Gee, I'd really like to upgrade our website this year", that's an *idea*. It's nice, but it hasn't committed you to any course of action.

However, if you write on a piece of paper the:

- <u>Objective</u> ("We will upgrade our website")
- <u>Rationale</u> ("because our site is looking outdated vs. our competitors")
- <u>Project leader</u>—who's responsible for the quality and completion of a project.
- <u>Timeline</u>—including the launch date and all intermediate due dates and
- <u>Budget</u>—for the entire project.

Now you've committed time, people and dollars to this project, and its likelihood of success has grown exponentially.

#2 – You can hang it in front of your nose

After you've finished your marketing plan, I recommend taping up parts of it all around you—maybe on your cubicle wall, on your computer monitor, or over your phone. The goal is to hang it where you'll see it every day. There are two reasons for this.

First, seeing it every day serves as a conscious reminder to get this week's tasks done. Yes, it's a subtle form of nagging, but I guarantee you'll get more done because of the subtle pressure you feel.

Second, having the plan in plain view helps 'sink' the plan into your subconscious. As your eye passes over the plan, your conscious mind may not notice. But, your subconscious mind does and starts acting upon it. Your subconscious mind is extremely powerful and is actually converting your plan into action 24 hours a day, 7 days a week. You don't consciously know it's happening, but it is.

The subconscious mind is too big a topic to cover here, but if you're interested in learning more about it, try reading *The Magic of Believing* by Claude Bristol.

#3 – A plan breaks down your effort into manageable chunks

When you develop a marketing plan, complete with an annual marketing timeline (see Chapter 11), you'll know, every Monday morning, *exactly* what you need to accomplish that week to stay on track. Furthermore, a marketing timeline takes a seemingly huge task (e.g. develop a website) and breaks it down into smaller and more manageable sub-tasks.

#4 – A plan gives you hope

With a completed marketing plan guiding your efforts, you'll be amazed at how much more confident you feel. Now, amidst all the day-to-day fire fighting, you'll know you have a plan, a path to follow, and a quiet assurance that you're building *momentum* for your business. That positive attitude alone goes a long way towards steering a company in the right direction.

#5 – Your marketing plan acts as an "idea sifter"

Over the course of 12 months (we'll assume you're writing an annual marketing plan here), you'll probably stumble across some marketing opportunity you didn't foresee when you wrote your plan. Maybe you get a call from a magazine offering you discounted advertising rates. Or you meet the president of a call center who offers its telemarketing services to your company. Maybe your printer, based upon previous successes with companies in your industry, suggests you try a direct mail campaign. Should you do these things?

With a written marketing plan in place, you can "sift" each idea through it. If you've spent thoughtful time developing your marketing strategies and committing them to paper, you'll know quickly if any of these ideas are on-strategy.

#6 – A plan gives you something to go back to in slow times

If your business is like most others, it has a seasonality to it. That is, some months are traditionally slower than others. During those slow months, instead of wringing your hands and worrying about slow sales, you know what to do. Crack open the plan, and review it cover to cover. Are your assumptions about the market still valid? Do your strategies still make sense? Which tactics do we need to implement?

At a glance, you can tell if you're ahead of schedule or behind, and turn reactive statements like "I don't know what I should do" into proactive statements like "We've planned a newsletter in the 2nd quarter, and now's the time" or "I need to pick up the pace on our website."

How long does it take to write a marketing plan?

It depends. How long it takes to write your marketing plan depends on these factors in your business:

- ○ Revenue size
- ○ Geographic scope
- ○ Distribution channels
- ○ Markets served
- ○ Number of products or services offered
- ○ Number of employees.

The larger the number of any of these variables, the longer it will take. As a general rule of thumb, a sole proprietor can write a marketing plan in 1-4 weeks. Not burdened with bosses or employees, the free-lancer has an open field in which to perform. Thus, you the free-lancer only have to manage your schedule and motivation to complete a marketing plan.

Larger companies will find that developing a marketing plan takes from 8-12 weeks. More time is needed because the larger company has to account for more people, more opinions and (usually) more complex operations.

Whichever situation you face, be sure to budget for enough think time— that is time away from the planning process itself where you can ruminate, cogitate or (if so inclined) meditate about the major questions you face.

Remember, the key to well-thought-out strategies is just that—thought. Sometimes, the most effective strategies need time to gel in others' minds.

When to start

When should you start your marketing plan for the next year? Let's assume your fiscal year starts in January. If you're a sole proprietor, you should start your market planning process right after Thanksgiving. If you're in a larger business, begin your market planning shortly after Labor Day.

Remember...

A marketing plan is a key component to more focused and directed thinking about your marketing. If you're really serious about your marketing, a plan is the best first step.

Tools To Go

- Effective marketing involves thinking before acting.
- A marketing plan:
  - Lays the groundwork for action
  - Can be hung in front of your nose
  - Breaks down the work into manageable chunks
  - Gives you hope
  - Acts as an idea sifter
  - Gives you something to go back to in slow times
- For smaller businesses, count on 4 weeks to develop the plan. Begin right after Thanksgiving.
- For larger businesses, 8-12 weeks is a better timeframe. Begin right after Labor Day.

"Begin with the
end in mind."

Steven Covey,
Author

Chapter 6

Your Business Vision & Goals: Keeping Your Eyes on the Prize

I remember reading in John Sculley's book, *Odyssey: Pepsi to Apple...a Journey of Adventure, Ideas & the Future,* how Steve Jobs, the then president of Apple Computers, sold him on the idea of working for Apple over Sculley's current employer, Pepsi-Cola. When it came time for Jobs to offer Sculley the position at Apple, he asked Sculley directly "What would you rather do—sell flavored water or change the world?" The idea of changing the world is a very compelling vision isn't it? It's so vivid and motivating that it's no wonder Apple made the impact it did.

You too must find a compelling vision for your business. Your vision statement must be vividly descriptive and move people to action. I recommend developing your vision statement with a 5-year timeframe in mind. In other words, your vision statement must answer the questions "What will this company be after 5 years?"

As you can probably imagine, developing your company's vision statement is not going to happen overnight. You'll want to account for lots of time to discuss, debate and reflect. After all, you're painting a picture of the future.

Developing your vision statement

Start by assembling all the key players in your company and brainstorming answers to the following questions:

1. What do we want to be known for in 5 years? What legacy do we want the company to leave?

_____

_____

_____

2. What business are we in?

_____

_____

_____

3. What markets do we want to dominate?

_____

_____

_____

4. What position do we want to occupy? #1? A leader? One of the leaders? A pioneer? A player?

_____

_____

_____

5. How far geographically do we want to cover?

_____

_____

_____

As these answers crystallize, compile as many of these elements into one or two sentence statements using different adjectives and nouns. They might look something like this:

"Emerge Marketing will be a leading, marketing firm that grows companies through great marketing"

OR

"Solid Foundations Masonry will be the driving force in the international foundations market."

The bolder and more memorable the mission statement, the better. Leading cosmetic company, Revlon, uses "We sell hope" as its vision statement. Now that's something your employees can get behind!

Spreading it far and wide

After you've finished the process and created a vision statement that all key leaders agree is powerful, distribute it to every employee in the company. I've found that two factors play a key role in how well a vision statement motivates a growing company's employees. They are:

1. How widely the vision statement is distributed.

Everyone in the company should receive a copy of it—from the president on down to the custodial staff. Let's face it, for any team to achieve its objectives, everyone on the team must know what it's trying to achieve.

2. How often it's communicated.

I see many companies with a vision statement that's buried in a file somewhere. For anything to seep into a company's culture and actions, it should be repeated over and over. The most successful growing companies I see consistently refer back to their vision statement. Use it in speeches, employee newsletters, presentations, employee meetings, intranets, employee parties—anywhere your employees are a captive audience.

How to set business goals

> *"This nation should commit itself to achieving the goal, before this decade is out, of landing a man on the moon and returning him safely to Earth."*
>
> John F. Kennedy, 1961

This is one of the most recognizable goals in all of American history, and when I watch tapes of JFK unveiling it, I still get goosebumps. When outlining this goal, he did everything right. He challenged a group of people with an attainable goal, and set a deadline. It's been written that "Goals are dreams with deadlines" and JFK's momentous words in the early '60's certainly lend credence to that idea.

Those growing businesses I work with, that have concrete goals, always seem to have a more definitive sense of purpose. It's clear in their minds what they're striving for, and they seem driven to achieve it. Those businesses without goals seem rudderless. So my advice here is, set goals for your business and watch how they quickly become your business' driving force.

The A-R-T of goal setting

Did you know there's an ART to developing goals? That's right, the 'A-R-T' of developing powerful goals is to make them:

- **A**ttainable (realistic)
- **R**esponsible (to someone)
- **T**rackable (with a deadline)

If your goals follow this simple formula, they will be crystal clear—and powerful motivators.

Hard Goals

Marketers have two kinds of goals: *hard goals* and *soft goals*. A hard goal is one that can be quantified and measured such as:

- Increase sales by $500,000 by December 31.
- Increase profits +15% by year end.
- Get 3 new customers in the first half.
- Roll-out 2 new products by the first quarter.
- Launch 3 new value-added services by June 1.
- Raise prices 5% on April 3.

When you reach the date you've set, you'll know whether or not you achieved it. That's what makes these hard goals so powerful.

Remember when you received your report card at school? At the end of a semester, you knew where you'd done well and where you hadn't. In short, you knew where you stood. It's the same with hard goals. At the end of your business year, you'll be able to measure a great deal of your marketing progress by whether or not you've achieved these hard goals.

To arrive at some hard goals for your business, try using this template I've developed. In it, you'll sketch out:

- <u>What</u> the goal is (Increase sales)
- <u>How much</u> you want to achieve (15%)
- <u>When</u> you want it achieved by (Dec 31, '02)
    and
- <u>Who</u> is responsible for achieving this goal (Marketing & Sales Team).

Now, in the grid below, try coming up with 3 hard goals that establish *what, how much, when* and *who* and jot them down:

What	How Much	By when	Whom
e.g. Emerge will increase its sales	15%	by 12/31/02	Marketing & Sales Team

Soft Goals

Unlike hard goals, you can't quantify soft goals. But, they're every bit as important as your hard ones. Here are some examples of soft goals:

- Increase company awareness this year.
- Improve our image in the first quarter.
- Strengthen our branding by 12/31.
- Develop our positioning by June 1.
- Educate the market on all our services by 12/31.

As you can see, these soft goals are more difficult to quantify. Here's a trick; to better define these soft goals, try finishing the phrase "so that..." after each of your goals. Doing so helps you spell out what impact this soft goal will then have on your company.

For example, you may say "We want to develop our company's positioning by June 1, so that *we differentiate ourselves from the competition*." The more you spell out the end benefit to your company, the better you'll recognize its impact.

Now, try coming up with 3 soft goals on your own and write them out here:

What	By when	So that	Whom
e.g. Emerge will improve its branding	by 12/31/01	a more consistent image results	Marketing & Sales Team

After you've defined your hard & soft goals for the upcoming year, you can move on to the problem-solving stage.

Remember...

Your vision and goals should be powerful and motivating. They are the distant 'prizes' you'll focus on throughout your marketing campaign. So, "keep your eyes on the prize" and let's move forward to the next stage of marketing planning.

Tools To Go

○ Effective marketing involves thinking before acting.
○ Your vision statement is your "prize". Keep your eyes on the prize.
○ After you've finished your vision statement, distribute it to everyone throughout your business.
○ Keep on communicating your vision long after you've completed it.
○ Make sure your goals are A-R-T (Attainable, Responsible and Trackable).
○ Work to identify both Hard (quantitative) & Soft (qualitative) goals.

"From error to error,
one discovers the
entire truth."

Sigmund Freud,
Psychoanalyst

Chapter 7

How To Identify Your Marketing Problems

Once during a workshop session I was leading, an attendee took issue with my use of the word "problem". It seems he'd been trained to call them "opportunities", and felt that my use of the word "problem" was negative. Now, I'm all for putting a positive spin on things, but in my mind problems are something we grow up with. Can you imagine how some of our day-to-day expressions might change if we substituted "opportunity" for "problem"? For example:

"Johnny, I've got an *opportunity* with your attitude."

"Susie, please finish your math *opportunities*."

"He's a real *opportunity* in the classroom."

I believe in telling it straight with a minimum of happy-talk, so in my world, you'll find "problems" in a marketing effort, and "opportunities" in the want ads section!

Marketing is a problem-solving exercise

At this stage in the development of your marketing plan, you'll identify all marketing problems (i.e. lack of awareness, declining sales, too-low pricing, etc.) your business faces, and get them out on the table. Then, you're going to prioritize each to determine which require immediate attention. Finally, you'll begin addressing those highest-priority problems.

How do you know what your problems are?

Back when you were assessing and researching your business, you probably identified some of your problems. Perhaps your employees kept mentioning that your prices were too high. Or maybe your customers complained that your product line wasn't broad enough. Maybe you noted a lack of awareness for your business.

Go back through your notes from both the market assessment and research efforts you've finished. Which problems did you hear repeatedly? What were the top concerns on most people's minds?

If nothing jumps out at you, here is a list of the most common problems we find in growing businesses:

The Most Common Marketing Problems

O Our market is shrinking.

O Our current customers are leaving.

O We're not generating new customers.

O No one knows who we are.

O The market thinks we offer only one product or service—but we offer so many more.

O We don't have a marketing plan.

O Our marketing is helter-skelter.

O We lack the staff to get our marketing done.

O Our profits are declining.

O We lack certain marketing tools (i.e. a brochure, a presentation).

O Our prices are too high (or too low).

O We're attracting the wrong kinds of customers.

O Our geographic scope is too limited.

O We sell only one product.

O We lack a consistent image or brand.

Scan this list and then check off two or three of your most persistent marketing problems. After you've identified them, record them here (leaving the priority space blank for the moment):

Marketing Problems:	
Marketing Problems	**Priority**

3-2-1

When I worked as marketing director at a $7 million company, my staff and I developed a project list with over 75 tasks on it! Seeking direction, I asked my boss which he saw as the most important. He answered "All of 'em." Hogwash! Don't fall into this trap of thinking everything is equally important. Instead, use a thoughtful prioritization process to help you weed out the urgent from the truly important.

Now that you've identified and recorded your key marketing problems above, go back and assign each one a priority using the following ranking system:

3 = Very Important
Must address in 6 months

2 = Important
Must address in less than 12 months

1 = Somewhat important
Can be addressed after 12 months

In this system, a problem rated as a "3" is a <u>very important</u> problem that must be addressed within six months. A "2" is an <u>important</u> problem that must be addressed within 12 months. And a "1" is a <u>somewhat important</u> problem that can be addressed after a year (or during the next planning season).

This system acknowledges upfront that *all* your problems are important, yet concedes some are more pressing than others.

If you have other folks involved in the development of your marketing plan—say committee members or task force members—simply have each person rank the problems individually. Then average everyone's ratings to come up with an average score.

For example, let's say your task force has identified "No marketing plan" as a problem. Four people rank it a 3, one ranks it a 2 and one ranks it a 1. The average value for this problem then is 2.5.

Furthermore, let's say your task force comes up with 4 other problems and ranks those accordingly. Your company's problem grid will now look like this:

Marketing Problems:	
Marketing Problems	**Priority**
• No marketing plan	2.5
• Outdated selling materials	2.3
• Prices are too low	2.0
• Marketing efforts sporadic	1.5
• Declining sales per customer	1.2

Now, you have a snapshot of your company's marketing problems, in priority order.

Remember...

If any step in the marketing process calls for candor, this is it. All subsequent marketing actions will be built around the problems you identify here. So, be honest. The truth hurts sometimes, but it can also set you free!

Tools To Go

○ Call them problems. That's what they are.

○ Generate a list of all key marketing problems and then prioritize them using the 3-2-1 system.

○ If you have others involved in your marketing plan, get their rankings, then average all the values.

○ Be honest.

"If you chase two rabbits,
both will escape."

Proverb

Chapter 8

Targeting: Who Are the Right Prospects for You?

If you asked me to identify the most important decision in a marketing effort—I'd say it's who you target. Think about it. Even if you possessed a breakthrough product, award-winning materials and a crack sales team, all of your efforts would fall on deaf ears if you were talking to the wrong people.

I'll give you two quick examples. I've been happily married for over 20 years, yet I still receive direct mail solicitations for a dating service! And, a friend of mine gets invitations to shop at a neighborhood pet superstore, yet he doesn't own a pet.

I think it's safe to say these ill-targeted marketing efforts are counter-productive. They annoy and antagonize the recipients and work to damage a company's reputation.

Correct targeting however, is a horse of a different color. If you've clearly identified your audience, the pain it feels and the solutions it seeks, your marketing is like a beacon in the darkness. People (and I mean here the right people) will naturally be drawn to it.

So, let's spend some time developing a comprehensive profile of your target audience.

B-2-B or B-2-C?

The first question you'll have to answer is "Do I sell to other businesses or to individual customers?" Those that sell to other businesses, are called business-to-business marketers (B2B), and those that sell to individual consumers are business-to-consumer (B2C) marketers. How you market your product or company will differ greatly based on whether you're a B2B or B2C marketer.

If you market to consumers

If you own a tanning salon, or a web-based collectibles company, or a coin operated laundromat, your primary purchasers are consumers. To help you hone in on a comprehensive profile of these customers, I recommend using the PAL approach.

This acronym is a handy way to remember the three most effective ways to identify these consumers. They are:

Profile
Affinity
Lifestyle

Profile – Your target's profile establishes the *demographics* of your audience. Demographics are statistics about the socioeconomic makeup of your audience and include:

- Age
- Gender
- Marital status
- Household size
- Presence of children
- Ages of children
- Ethnic group
- Education
- Occupation
- Religion
- Principle language spoken
- Home ownership
- Type of car owned

Using 2 or 3 of these categories, see if you can define your audience in a single sentence. Maybe it's as simple as saying your audience is *"Married, stay-at-home moms with preschool children"* or *"Spanish speaking males, aged 35-54 with full-time jobs"*.

Affinity – Once you've established a better profile of your audience, try to uncover the significant affiliations (or relationships) in their lives. These are called *affinities* and might include:

- Grade schools & high schools attended
- Colleges attended
- Advanced degree programs
- Church affiliation
- Fraternal organizations (e.g. Kiwanis)
- Service organizations (e.g. VFW)
- Fraternities/sororities
- Clubs
- Community groups
- Recreational teams
- Employers

For example, if you talk to me as a white male in his forties, then I listen with one ear. But if you talk to me as a member of the Sigma Phi Epsilon fraternity, of which I'm a member, now you have my full attention.

Location – One other effective way to target, especially for smaller businesses, is geographically. Depending upon your business' ability to deliver its products and services, your targeting location could be as small as a 3-block radius around your store, or as geographically broad as the entire world.

Here are some common geographic areas used in targeting:

- Block
- Postal carrier route
- Neighborhood
- Zip code
- City
- Metropolitan Statistical Area (MSA)
- State
- County
- Country

To target is to focus

Remember that targeting specific groups of consumers is a way to make your marketing efforts more efficient. Instead of talking to everybody, you've now identified niches. This decision alone will save your marketing effort time and valuable money, and force you to focus even further on the needs and wants of this audience.

What if you market to businesses?

Now, if you sell to other businesses, you go about targeting in a different fashion altogether. Here your targeting must take on two dimensions. You'll not only research and profile the businesses you're targeting (e.g. midwestern wood manufacturers), but you'll also uncover the key characteristics of the purchasers within these businesses.

So, the first 3 questions you'll have in the B2B targeting process are:
1. What <u>types</u> of businesses do we target?
2. Who are the <u>decision-makers</u> in each?
   and
3. Who are the <u>gatekeepers</u> to a purchase decision?

We'll now go into more depth for each one.

Profiling your target businesses

When I ask our clients the question *"What kinds of businesses do you sell to?"* I very often get the answer *"All kinds"*—and that's perfectly normal. But when I follow that question up with *"Which of these businesses are the <u>best fit</u> for your product?"*, I'm often greeted with blank stares. You see, many companies chase after any and all customers. And to be perfectly honest, I made the same mistake when starting our business. I actively pursued Fortune 500 businesses, mid-sized businesses and even 1 person, free-lance businesses. It didn't matter to me as long as they paid on time!

After a while though, my customers got confused, and had trouble referring me business. And I found them asking me the question "Which businesses are the best fit for *your* service?"

To help you find these that fit best, use one or all of these 3 criteria to begin your targeting efforts:

1. Standard Industrial Classification (SIC) codes
2. Company size
3. Geography

Targeting businesses using SIC Codes

Today in 2002, there are over 12 million businesses in the U.S., and each is assigned a standard industrial classification (SIC) code. This code, which can be up to eight digits long, is used by the U.S. Government to identify the primary activity of each business.

Some examples of current SIC codes are:

- 2434-01 is Wood-Kitchen Cabinets
- 8888-07 is Work-at-Home Businesses
- 5087-26 is Laundry-Equipment (Wholesale)

I should say at the outset that the U.S. Standard Industrial Classification (SIC) system is being replaced by The North American Industry Classification System (NAICS). The NAICS system was developed jointly by the U.S., Canada, and Mexico to provide new comparability in statistics about business activity across North America. However, as of this writing in 2002, the SIC system is still widely used for list purchasing or database queries. For more information about SIC codes you can visit www.osha.gov/oshstats/sicser.html and for more information about the NAICS system, visit www.census.gov/epcd/www/naics./html.

Here are a couple things to remember about SIC codes. First, understand that a listing of companies in one SIC code is not a comprehensive list. It's simply a list of all known companies with this code.

Also remember that one company may have several SIC codes assigned to it. Companies with subsidiaries, diversified operations or vertical integration may have several SIC codes assigned to them. Be aware of this as you start using SIC codes for your targeting. If you're interested in purchasing lists of companies using SIC codes, visit www.infousa.com or www.zapdata.com

Using company size

You can also target certain businesses by their size. The two most effective ways to target by size are by company revenues and by employee count.

Let's say you offered outsourced human resource services. You may determine that companies with revenues in the range of $2-20 million are a best fit for you. Companies of that size have human resource issues, yet lack the capital to hire a full-time human resources person. Knowing that this revenue range best describes your target, you can better qualify prospects as you talk to them.

Here's another example. If you sell a product to home based businesses, you know that these are largely 1-person companies. Now, when you buy a mailing list you can really narrow your focus to just those 1-person companies in your market.

Targeting businesses by geography

You could also target your customers geographically. When I launched our business in the early 90's, I remember a friend of mine advising me to concentrate on companies outside the metro area where I lived. He reasoned that, with such heated competition inside the metro area, anyone who concentrated outside the metro area would find a target audience largely ignored by the competition.

I must admit that, with clients who quickly sprang up in the metro area, I didn't follow his advice. But ever since then I was keenly aware of the role that geography plays in targeting your audience.

Who are the decision-makers?

If your company sells to businesses, it's easy to think that the only detailed profiling you'll do concerns the companies you're selling to. But that's not true. You want to also profile the people you sell to within those businesses, and you may find that there are several people involved in the decision to buy your company's products. So, who inside a company typically approves purchases of your product? Is it the Purchasing Manager? VP of Marketing? CEO? Chief Financial Officer? Personnel clerk? Several of these?

When you dig into this question, you may be surprised at the answers. One client of ours, for example, manufactures thermoformed-plastic packaging. They initially thought Purchasing Managers were their target. But after conducting some basic research, they found that Product Designers were the true decision-makers for their products. It turned out that one area my client really excelled at was engineering a package design so that it solved a particular packaging problem. Once my client demonstrated their engineering expertise to the Product Designer, they were sold on doing business with my client. As a result, the Designers would approach the Purchasing department and sell them on using my client. In a situation like this, it was very hard for the Purchasing folks to use any other plastics manufacturer.

Back when I sold mainframe software packages, I learned that the people who carried sway for this product were the users of the computer software— data entry clerks, accounting supervisors and accountants. After all, they'd use the software every day, and it proved to be a major tool in their day-to-day jobs.

If the users weren't convinced of my software's superiority, Purchasing wouldn't ask me back. From this learning, I realized that most of my selling efforts would have to be targeted at end users, rather than the purchasing department. To get at whom you target within a company, answer these questions:

1. Which department(s) and job titles will actually use the product (or service) you provide?

1) _____

2) _____

3) _____

2. Which peoples' job performances are directly affected by using your product?

1) _____

2) _____

3) _____

3. Is there a committee that must approve purchases of your product or service? If so, who sits on that committee?

1) _____

2) _____

3) _____

Once you identify and prioritize which people you'll target, you'll naturally begin to formulate your selling strategy. It could be as simple as "Meet with the users first, then talk to purchasing, and after that present to the committee." But, a little research into the buying habits within your target companies will go a long way towards closing sales later on in your marketing effort.

Don't forget the gatekeepers

When I marketed a kids cereal brand, I learned all about *gatekeepers*.
As part of our marketing research efforts, I would go into grocery stores and
observe families shopping in the cereal aisle.

I'd watch a young child pick up a box of cereal, perhaps recognizing the
product mascot from a Saturday morning TV commercial. Then the child
would drag it over to her mother for approval. Sometimes, the mother smiled
lovingly back at the child and put the box in the shopping cart. But more
often than not, she'd make a face and say something like "No honey, I don't
think we can get you this one. How about this one instead?" while reaching
for another. I didn't realize it at the time, but this was my first experience
with gatekeepers.

The mother, as you've guessed by now, was the gatekeeper. Without her
approval, the customer (the child) wouldn't buy our product. In business-to-
business transactions, a gatekeeper acts in much the same way, wielding
considerable influence over the purchase decision, while not actually using
the product.

You'll find gatekeepers throughout all marketing and selling efforts. In my
previous software example, the Chief Financial Officer was the gatekeeper
for the software purchase. A CEO might act as a gatekeeper for a large-scale
machinery purchase. The Vice President of Marketing could be a gatekeeper
when hiring a graphic design firm.

Learn who the gatekeepers are for your products and then work to understand exactly what they look for in a product like yours. Many times you'll
find it's something quite different from those people who end up using the
product.

Develop a target profile

After you gather together this information on your target, you'll want to
distill it down to a pithy 30-words-or-less profile of this target. It might look
like this:

Our target is:

> *"Purchasing personnel for Fortune 500 manufacturers who purchase widgets from AAA certified vendors."*
>
> OR
>
> *"Stay-at-home moms in the U.S., who feel stressed for time and want to save themselves time and hassles."*
>
> OR
>
> *"CEO's of U.S. companies with sales between $1 - $50 million and employee counts between 10-100."*

Now, paint a picture

One day in the 80's, I sat in a graduate school marketing class, and the professor asked us to describe what the male consumer of a Seagram's Wine Cooler® looked like. The class then painted a picture of a young, clean-shaven, urban professional who wore a 3-piece suit, wingtips and a conservative tie.

Then, the professor asked us to describe the consumer for a Bartles & Jaymes Wine Cooler®. This time, we painted a picture of an unshaven surfer-dude wearing a floral shirt, shorts and sandals. Wow, what different people these two guys were!

Yet, if we'd relied on just demographics to describe each, the class would have lumped them together into the "white, 20-something, male" category. These two people's demographics were the same, yet their lifestyles and behaviors were as different as night and day.

That's why your targeting effort isn't really complete until you develop a *minds-eye picture* of your target. This is a written description that captures the lifestyle, thoughts and emotions of your target audience.

To help you with this, here are some questions:

○ Who are these people, really? What do they look like? How do they think and act?

○ What do they lack? (e.g. time, money, resources, friends)

○ How are they feeling?

○ What is preventing them from succeeding—or being happy?

○ What solution(s) specifically are they looking for?

○ If they had your product/service, how would their life be different?

The trick is to tell a mini-story as you're writing the mind's-eye picture. This story should be so vivid and genuine that the reader commiserates, with every bone in her body, the situation this person faces.

Here's an actual minds-eye picture I developed for a travel industry client. It describes a working mom and the pain she feels when planning a vacation:

Mind's Eye Picture – Example

"Today's world is different. I'm under constant pressure—time pressures, financial pressures and the pressure to balance work & family.

Funny how planning a vacation just adds more pressure to my life. I have to research all the options and follow up on all the details. It's all up to me to find the right things to do on a limited budget. And even then, the pressure's still on because my husband may not like what I've planned.

With one phone call, I want to talk to a knowledgeable travel agent who'll save me time and money and take care of all the details."

What you'll get from this exercise is an *emotional* feeling for your target. Knowing *who* they are is important. But knowing how they *feel* takes you much deeper. Most purchase decisions are based on emotions, so once you can uncover your prospect's pain, and fully understand the emotions behind it, you can more accurately target your messages and speak directly to this pain.

Know who's in the middle

Let's suppose for a moment that you manufacture a product. You then sell it to a distributor who in turn, sells it to retail stores, where the customer buys it.

The distributor and retailers in this scenario are called *intermediaries*. They're partners in the warehousing, distribution and promotion of your product, and as a result, are really the first customers of your product. That's because without their approval, your product would never make it into the hands of the end consumer.

Therefore, it goes without saying that you must profile these intermediaries as well. Remember, without them, your product never ends up in the hands of those using it, so you must sell these intermediaries first. To help you do so, rough out a P-A-L analysis (described earlier) for each.

The most commonly found intermediaries are:
• Distributors
• Wholesalers
• Brokers
• Manufacturer reps
• Dealers
     and
• Value-added resellers.

Spend time profiling them as you would the end consumer for your product and you'll be well on your way to higher sales.

Remember...

Spend a great deal of time profiling your end consumers and intermediaries. This is no time to scrimp on research time and effort. Clear and concise thinking about who these people are and what motivates them will save you a great deal of time (and money) later on.

Tools To Go

○ Targeting is the single most important marketing decision you'll make—spend quality time on it.

○ Determine if your company is a business-to-business (B2B) or business-to-consumer (B2C) marketer.

○ Use the P-A-L (Profile, Affinity, Lifestyle) approach to characterize your prospects.

○ If your company is B2B, then profile the companies and people within them that you'll target.

○ Develop a Minds-Eye Picture of those you target.

"Strategy and timing are
the Himalayas of marketing.
Everything else is
the Catskills."

Al Ries & Jack Trout,
Authors

Chapter 9

Marketing Strategies: The Key Thrusts of Your Plan

Imagine for a moment you're a soldier in the army and your commanding officer approaches. He gathers together the troops in your company and then announces:

"Troops, we're going to take Hill 436 today. **(Goal)**

We're going to first soften up the opposition with air strikes, and then immediately follow that up with a west-side artillery attack and a south-side infantry attack. **(Strategies)**

At 14:00 the air strikes will commence using precision guided missiles, the artillery will then attack from the west at 15:00 using missile launchers and howitzers and at 15:10 the infantry will attack via the south access road using small arms and grenades." **(Tactics)**

As I've noted above, the strategies are in the second paragraph, the goal is in the first and the tactics in the third. From this description, you can more clearly discern the difference between goals, strategies and tactics. When you compare the strategies statement above with the other statements, you'll see that a strategy is a broad directional thrust you'll take while tactics are much more detailed. In fact, the word strategy comes from the Greek root *strategia* meaning "act of a general." Contrast that with the word tactic, which comes from the root *taktakia*, meaning "the art of arranging."

Write strategies that include action-oriented words

If strategies help accomplish goals then, by their very nature, they must be action oriented. So, it's important to word your strategies to encourage action. I've found that leading off all strategies with action-oriented words is a good first step.

As you begin formulating your strategies, try beginning each strategy with action-oriented verbs like these:

Action-oriented verbs:

- O Coordinate
- O Improve
- O Plan
- O Execute
- O Complete
- O Develop
- O Restructure
- O Research

- O Investigate
- O Upgrade
- O Design
- O Acquire
- O Obtain
- O Quantify
- O Analyze

For example, which of these is a stronger strategy statement?:
Upgrade current selling materials OR *Selling materials*

Define the desired outcome

The second portion of a strategy statement lines out the desired outcome. How do you do this? Simply complete the strategy statement using the *phrase "so that…"* or *"in order to…"*. This helps you focus on what impact the strategy will have on your business.

So, in the example above, the strategy *"Upgrade current selling materials"* would now be written as:

> *"Upgrade current selling materials <u>so that</u> we develop a more contemporary image."*

Leave no doubt about the anticipated aim of each strategy.

Strategies attack problems

If you're having trouble developing your strategies, go back to the marketing problems you identified earlier. Here again, from Chapter 7, is a list of the most common marketing problems I run into:

The most common marketing problems

○ Our market is shrinking.

○ Our current customers are leaving.

○ We're not generating new customers.

○ No one knows who we are.

○ The market thinks we offer only one product or service— but we offer so many more.

○ We don't have a marketing plan.

○ Our marketing is helter-skelter.

○ We lack the staff to get our marketing done.

○ Our profits are declining.

○ We lack certain marketing tools (i.e. a brochure, a presentation).

○ Our prices are too high (or too low).

○ We're attracting the wrong kinds of customers.

○ Our geographic scope is too limited.

○ We sell only one product.

○ We lack a consistent image or brand.

If any of these problems jump out at you, then in all likelihood you'll want to develop strategies to attack them head-on.

Strategies also come from your goals

Now, go back and review the goals you set in Chapter 6. Some of your strategies will be natural outgrowths of these. For example, if you set the goal, *Acquire 5 new clients by December 31*, it's only natural that marketing strategies will evolve from that goal. One strategy could be: "Increase networking activities so that we generate more referrals." Or your strategy instead might be: "Launch a direct mail campaign targeted at new businesses so that we increase our prospect base."

Understand where your target gets its information

For many promotional strategies, a helpful exercise is to first identify where your target audience gets its information. That is, where does your target go to find out more about your product or service? Magazines? Newspapers? Trade shows? Websites? Conferences or networking events? Some of us are avid readers, others love to meet peers face-to-face at trade events, and still others prefer surfing the web. All these are valid information gathering methods, but you as the marketer must dig a little deeper by asking:

- **What <u>offline</u> publications does my target read?**

_____

_____

_____

- **What <u>online</u> publications do they read?**

_____

_____

_____

- **What media do they watch?**

_____

_____

_____

_____

- **Where do they congregate with others like themselves? (e.g. conferences, seminars, trade shows, events)**

_____

_____

_____

_____

- **Who are the opinion leaders they seek out? (e.g. industry experts, consultants, media members)**

_____

_____

_____

_____

After you've tackled these questions, you may end up uncovering marketing vehicles that form the basis for a strategy. For example, if you answered that _Widgets USA_ and _E-Widgets.com_ were offline and online publications that your target reads religiously, then your next step would be to contact these publications for more information about their readership. A media kit from most publications will yield a wealth of information about that publication's readership, as well as current industry information. I'd want to know specifically if these publications were subscribed to in big enough numbers to make them worthwhile as a promotional vehicle.

Strategies should reflect your company personality

Is your company bold or laid-back? Outgoing or inwardly-focused? Aggressive or conservative? As you begin developing your marketing strategies, take a moment to consider if they're in keeping with your company's personality.

Let's say you decide you want to embark upon an aggressive telemarketing strategy to obtain new leads. If your company has historically been an inwardly focused company (say, a programming firm), this strategy may be at odds with your culture. Your employees may be reluctant to cold call for leads. Or, there may be a backlash among your prospect base because this practice is frowned upon in this industry.

Whatever the case, a marketing strategy that's incongruent with your company or industry culture will do more harm than good.

Strategizing your P's

Remember earlier we said the 4 P's of marketing were Price, Product, Place and Promotion? Since these cover the lion's share of marketing efforts, you should at least consider strategies for each. You may decide you don't need a pricing strategy—that's fine. But at least you've considered the option of a strategy and that's just being thorough.

A multitude of strategies

If there was a simple formula to develop marketing strategies, we wouldn't need marketers. You'd just plug in the variables, spit out the strategy, and move on to other things. But, developing marketing strategies involves sifting through all the options, weighing the pro's and con's and then picking the best strategy for the moment.

Take pricing for example. If we just asked the strategic question "What should our pricing strategy be?", there are a considerable number of options:

- Highest market price
- Price in the highest tier
- Price in the middle market tier
- Price in the lower market tier
- Everyday low price (ELP)
- Zone pricing
- Quantity pricing
- Trial pricing
- Price discounting

As you can see here, there are many strategies to choose from, and several could be viable options. To arrive at your final strategy in this example, I'd recommend choosing 2 or 3 possible strategies and then identifying the pro's and cons for each. After doing this for your top 2 or 3 options, you'll have a clearer picture of which strategy fits best. In the end, your final strategy will be a by-product of deliberate and thorough analysis—and that's good marketing!

Include your rationale

As your strategies take shape, each one should have supporting rationale behind it. *Rationale* is simply a succinct narration—a sentence or two— of *why* you've chosen this particular strategy. When you record this strategy, and include complete rationale for it, you:

- Establish your logic pattern for the strategy.
- Help others (e.g. executives, upper management, subordinates, new hires) understand why that strategy was chosen.
- Show you've done your homework.

Here's how a written strategy, followed by its rationale might look:

Strategy:

Develop e-commerce website so that the product line can broaden its sales channel.

Rationale:

1) We've reached our offline market saturation point.
2) Our primary competitors all have e-commerce sites.
3) Customer purchases by e-commerce sites are rising 15% annually.

Developing pricing strategies

Earlier in the chapter I shared a partial list of pricing strategies. Here is a more complete list:

Possible Pricing Strategies

- Highest market price
- Price in the highest tier
- Price in the middle market tier
- Price in the lower market tier
- Everyday low price (ELP)
- Zone pricing
- Quantity pricing
- Segmented by time of purchase (e.g. matinee tickets)
- Product bundling
- Loyal customer pricing
- Trial pricing
- Price discounting
- Trade dealing

Now, to narrow your options down, consider these questions:

- **Where does your current pricing strategy fall within this list?**

_____

_____

_____

- **Do your current prices provide acceptable margins?**

_____

_____

_____

- **Are your current prices competitive with your key competitors?**

_____

_____

_____

_____

- **How do your customers and prospects perceive your prices?**
  Do customers feel they're getting acceptable value for the price?

_____

_____

_____

_____

_____

If you have multiple products or serve multiple markets, you'll want to identify pricing strategies for each product line or market. They may be the same—they may not.

After answering these questions, your pricing strategy may end up looking like this:

Pricing Strategy:

We will seek highest market tier pricing for all our products to distinguish our products from the competition.

Rationale:

1. Positions us as higher quality than most competitors.
2. Further justifies some of our value-added services.
3. Ensures adequate margins now and in the future.

Developing product strategies

Here are some of the more common product strategies:

> ### *Possible Product (or Service) Strategies*
>
> O Expand existing product line.
> O Prune current product line.
> O Reduce product size.
> O Spin-off products to a separate line.
> O Bundle products together.
> O Upgrade product quality.
> O Augment the product with value-added services.
> O Improve packaging.
> O Reposition the product(s) or product line.
> O Offer trial sizes.

And to help winnow down these choices, consider these questions:

1. How (if at all) do your current products differ from your competitors'?

_____

_____

_____

_____

2. What additional products (or services) must you have in order to stay competitive in the market?

_____

_____

_____

_____

3. What additional products (or services), if you had them, would allow you to <u>leapfrog</u> the competition?

_____

_____

_____

_____

4. What improvements can you make to existing products (or services) to expand your business from current customers?

_____

_____

_____

_____

5. If contemplating a new market, what new products (or services) will you need?

_____

_____

_____

_____

6. What packaging improvements could you make to enhance your product's (or service's) value?

_____

_____

_____

_____

7. Which value-added services (or products) could you incorporate to improve your product's (or service's) appeal?

_____

_____

_____

_____

As you ponder product strategies, pay particular attention to the various product categories your company covers. I see a lot of companies out there, that define their offerings too broadly. Let me give you an example.

Let's say you have an accounting firm. When prospects ask what kind of business you're in, you answer "Accounting Services", period. This is a pretty general description of what you offer, but as a marketer, you must go deeper than this. Consider how much more interest you'd generate if you broadened that definition to include:

- We develop financial audits for small and mid-sized businesses.
- We prepare tax returns for busy executives.
- We perform due diligence for business buyers.
- We conduct business appraisals for buyers and sellers.
- We develop financial plans for accredited investors.

Do you see what I've done? I've called out specific products and the actual audience each appeals to. Now, prospects who hear these product definitions, stand a better chance of singling out themselves or others as prospects. Hearing (or reading) these more elaborate descriptions, they're more apt to say to themselves:

— _"I'm an accredited investor, maybe I need a financial plan."_ OR

— _"I'm a busy executive, maybe I could save a little time by having someone else prepare my tax return."_ OR

— _"I'm not thinking of selling my business, but a woman in my networking group is. Maybe I should refer you to her."_

How about another example? Let's say you manufacture wood components, and you tell buyers "We machine wood parts." That's a good start. But most wood parts buyers have specific problems they're trying to fix and, maybe the reason you're sitting across from this buyer today is that he needs to fix one of his problems...fast.

To spark more interest, try highlighting specific products like:

• Subassemblies for point of purchase displays.
• Wooden store fixtures for big-box retailers.
• Shelving for residential furniture units.

Remember, the more quickly you can spark a conversation about how your company will solve your buyer's problems, the faster you'll close the sale.

Developing distribution strategies

Here are some distribution strategy options to consider:

Possible Distribution Strategies

○ Expand into a new distribution channel.
○ Add/prune intermediaries.
○ Add/prune warehousing capacity.
○ Outsource core product/service elements (i.e. customer service, distribution)

○ Move operations to the Internet.
○ Expand domestically.
○ Expand internationally.

And to help narrow your choices for these strategies consider:

1. Which of your markets are underserved due to a lack of distribution?

_____

_____

_____

2. What distribution outlets or strategies are your competitors using against you to create a competitive advantage?

_____

_____

_____

_____

3. Can your products or services be sold via the Internet? Can they be delivered through the Internet? If so, is this one way to expand your distribution?

_____

_____

_____

_____

4. What new geographic markets afford you an opportunity to profitably grow?

_____

_____

_____

_____

A final note: The need for integration

Marketing integration is the process of making sure all your strategies fit and work together to maximize their impact.

For example, if you chose the product strategy _"Develop an upscale coffee and back it up with a price leader strategy and a promotional campaign in high-end food magazines,"_ this could all be torpedoed by distributing the product through discount stores.

After you've listed all strategies, go down your list and ask yourself of each one: *"Does this strategy link naturally with all our other strategies?"*

If you can answer yes to all strategies, you're well on your way to an integrated set of strategies

Remember...

Strategies are a key element of marketing. Just recently I read a brief story about a pharmaceutical company that hammered home the point. The 3rd quarter profits for this company, which was founded on delivering generic drugs, rose 1,067% (no, this is not a typo)! And, what happened to the stock price? It tanked 19 points—or 39% of its total market value! Why? The answer could be found in the next sentence of the story: *"The firm said it plans to focus on branded products that have higher profit margins instead of the tough generic drug business."* This was such a drastic and unexpected change in marketing strategy, that it caused over 1/3 of the company's total value to vanish overnight.

Choose your strategies carefully, only after a great deal of thought and discussion. They'll define your company for years to come.

Tools To Go

- ❍ Find Strategies in your problems & goals.
- ❍ Research where your target gets its information—there could be a strategy there.
- ❍ Synch your strategies with your company (and industry) personality.
- ❍ Strategize for all 4 P's—price, product, place and promotion.
- ❍ Include rationale for every strategy.
- ❍ Make sure your final strategies are well integrated.

14 Marketing vehicles plus their advantages & disadvantages

	Advantages	Disadvantages
Newspaper Ads	• Large readerships • Can target geographic areas • Split-run tests are available • Fast closings—can provide immediate exposure • Offers deep penetration	• Cluttered environment • Poor graphic quality • Most ads feature a sales/price orientation • Short-shelf life • Wasted circulation • Highly visible medium—competition can quickly react
Magazine Ads	• More targeted vehicle • Long shelf life • Higher reader involvement • Good for color • Better graphic quality	• Long lead times • Higher space costs vs. newspapers • Higher creative costs • Smaller audiences
Yellow Pages	• Reaches those ready-to-buy • Reasonably inexpensive • Can more easily track responses	• Listed right next to competitors—encourages price shopping • Creativity is restricted
Television Ads	• Huge reach • Offers sight, sound & motion • Good image-building medium	• Large creative & production costs • Preferred airtimes are often booked well in advance • Somewhat limited time constraints

	Advantages	**Disadvantages**
Cable TV Ads	• More affordable than television • Targeted audiences	• Smaller audiences • Suspect quality of some stations
Radio Advertising	• Universal medium—listened to throughout the day • Better targeted vehicle • Creates personality for a company • Some free creative help available • Rates can be negotiated	• Station-jumping means you must blanket the medium • Listeners can't refer back to your ads • Intrusive medium—needs repeating over & over • Background medium
Direct Mail	• Message is targeted to those most likely to buy • Not constrained on length of message • Can be personalized • Keeps new marketing info from competitors longer • Can split test	• Long lead times • Must coordinate services of many (e.g. graphics, production, printing, mail) • Hard to keep mailing lists up to date • Usually requires follow-up (e.g. telemarketing)
Billboards	• Very cost efficient • Great for increasing awareness	• Message must be very short • Mnemonic phone numbers necessary (800-4Emerge)

14 Marketing vehicles...continued

	Advantages	Disadvantages
Telemarketing	• Cost effective compared to face-to-face sales • Can navigate through a company to find the right person • Results can be more easily measured and tracked • Can gather information for database efforts	• Intrusive • Poor image builder • Must be handled professionally with scripting & professionals
Internet	• Can instantly update content • Can be measured & analyzed more effectively • Provides worldwide presence, overnight • Establishes credibility faster for smaller companies	• Some people are technophobes — although this is changing • Requires professionals for set up & maintenance • Time investment to manage set-up, maintenance & upgrading
Publicity	• Establishes good credibility • Reprints (articles, interviews, etc) can be reused in selling process • Can drive traffic to website • Can create unexpected & unanticipated opportunities • Can earn community goodwill	• Longer lead times • No guarantees that releases will get picked up • Lack total creative control

14 Marketing vehicles...continued

	Advantages	Disadvantages
Trade Shows	• Provides dynamic & personal selling environment • Can demonstrate product • Can scope out the competition • Gets sales & marketing people out into the market • Allows networking	• Can be expensive (i.e. travel expenses, staff time, planning time) • Must conform to show's rules & specifications • Must be supported by training effort • Trade shows have a lifecycle • Bigger trade shows offer cluttered, fatiguing environment
Event Marketing	• Helps establish relationships • You retain creative control • Good events incorporate additional 'spin' (e.g. press releases, media attention)	• Heavy in-house planning load if you're building the event from scratch • It takes time to build loyalty & awareness for a new event • Difficult to measure & evaluate
Direct Sales	• Provides dynamic & personal selling environment • Allows problem solving • Provides a company face • Allows for networking & information gathering	• Overhead expense incurred • Ongoing management needed • Ongoing training needed

"If your train's on the wrong track, every station you come to is the wrong station."

Bernard Malamud,
Writer

Chapter 10

How To Develop Marketing Tactics That Drive Your Business Forward

When we discuss tactics with our clients, we describe them as "where the rubber meets the road."

That's because all the thinking, all the planning, all the strategizing comes down to your tactics. They're what you roll out into your market, and so they're what your customers see. In this sense, they're a reflection of your company—and you want this reflection to be the very best it can be.

That's why internally, your tactics have to be planned out so completely, so thoroughly, that there's absolutely no doubt about how they'll get accomplished. How do you get to your final tactics? Read on…

Brainstorming possible tactics

From your research and analysis up to this point, you've learned much about whom you're targeting, what products and prices they're looking for, and the best distribution channels to offer them through. Now the nitty-gritty takes place.

Your next step is to line up a brainstorm meeting where the attendees will be all people responsible for executing these future marketing programs. The purpose of this meeting is to generate a wide variety of tactical options to support your strategies.

So for example, if you've developed the strategy *Participate in trade shows*, then at this meeting you'll ask and answer questions like: Which trade shows should we exhibit at? How often should we exhibit at trade shows? Where are the most popular trade shows? Go back to your final strategies and for each one, try to generate at least three possible tactics to achieve each strategy.

To encourage the brainstorming process, keep in mind these brainstorming rules:

1. Your objective is to generate *possible* tactics—not decide upon any of them.

2. There aren't any bad ideas—every idea is a good idea at this stage.

3. Everyone must contribute ideas.

4. Use an outside facilitator if this will be a big job. If you have multiple products or divisions, sophisticated marketing channels or programs or just plain friction between folks, it's best to let a third-party person do the facilitating.

ABC them!

After you've finished generating possible tactics for each strategy, now prioritize them. To help with this I'd suggest two things. First, ask yourself these questions when prioritizing tactics:

• Does this tactic clearly help accomplish the strategy?

• Do we have the people resources available, right now, to start and finish this tactic?

• Will this tactic make us somehow more unique in the marketplace?

Now, after covering these questions for all tactics, try using the following A-B-C scale to prioritize each one.

A	**B**	**C**
On Strategy	**Somewhat On Strategy**	**Off Strategy**
a tactic that fully supports a strategy (100%)	a tactic that somewhat supports a strategy (50%)	a tactic that doesn't support a strategy (0%)

Using these two steps, you should be able to winnow down your best marketing tactics to pursue.

Fleshing out the nitty-gritty's

Any brilliantly conceived tactic will be a dismal failure if it's poorly implemented. Therefore, it's your job at this point to carefully identify all the "nitty-gritty's" for each tactic.

To help you with these details behind each tactic, you'll need to answer these questions:

Tactical Nitty Gritty's

- ○ <u>What</u> is the tactic?
- ○ <u>When</u> will you do it?
- ○ <u>Who</u> will implement it?
- ○ <u>What</u> are the intermediate tasks to make this happen?
- ○ <u>How often</u> will you do it?
- ○ <u>How much</u> will it cost?

The more you completely think through these factors, the fewer surprises you'll encounter later on.

As you start filling in these fine points, another thing will happen. You'll start mentally allocating the people, time and money you need to accomplish tactics.

Plant the flag

When I worked at a large consumer products company, many times I'd find myself in market planning sessions where we were busy planning out a tactic. Sooner or later the discussion would reach a point where we'd have to make a decision about when the tactic would run. I call this the time to "Plant the Flag."

When you plant the flag, you commit—without any hesitation—to the date you want the public to first see (or learn about) a new marketing initiative of yours. This is called the *launch date*.

Let's say, for example, you've decided to send out a newsletter to your customers and prospects. To arrive at your launch date, you would ask yourself, "When do I want the first one in my customers' hands?" This then is your launch date.

Using a tactics list

As you start establishing tactics and their launch dates, I suggest you capture that information in a *tactics list*.

A tactics list is a planning device to help you record the key details for each of your tactics. Let's take an example. Say you've decided to host an Open House and you've set 6/02 as the launch date for it—in this case, the date of the actual Open House. After establishing these two things, enter them into your tactics list, so it looks like this:

Tactics List			
Tactic	**Launch Date**	**Who**	**How Much**
Develop Open House	6/1/02		

Next step: assigning a "who"

Every tactic must have a project leader to make sure the project is accomplished. The next step for you is to establish <u>who</u> the project leader for this tactic will be.

In smaller businesses, this usually ends up being the one (and only!) person responsible for the marketing effort. In larger businesses however, this person can vary. It might be one of your subordinates, it might be you, or it could even be someone outside the marketing department. In another chapter I'll give you some ideas and tips on deciding who might be the best project leader for any of your tactics. In the meantime, let's assume you already know who will lead this tactic; add their name to your tactics list.

How to establish a budget for a tactic

The last step in filling out your tactics list is to assign a budget number to each of your tactics. I'm always a little surprised at the number of clients who can't answer the question "How much have you budgeted for this project?" Budgeting for each tactic is a very important step, and not one to gloss over. If you don't do this, you may find yourself quickly overspent (in both the monetary <u>and</u> emotional senses of the word!).

There's a real art to establishing budgets. In fact, to me it's a kind of visualizing exercise. You have to visualize all aspects of the task to arrive at an accurate budget number. First, you break the tactic down into its distinct phases. Then, after costing out each distinct phase, you add up all the numbers to arrive at your total budget for the tactic.

Let's go back to the Open House example we had before. That's your tactic. Now, to get to a total budget number for this tactic, you're going to have to close your eyes and visualize its distinct phases.

They might be:
- O Pre-Open House Preparation
- O The Open House Event
- O Post-Open House Follow-up

From this exercise, you can identify some of the expense catagories for each phase like this:

Pre-Open House Preparation
O Invitations   O Event publicity
O Signage

The Open House Event
O Catering   O Brochures/flyers
O Demonstrations, speeches
O Prizes, giveaways, samples

Post-Open House Follow Up
O Thank you notes   O Sales rep calls
O Feedback forms

After you've costed out each of the tasks under the individual phases, you'll be more apt to arrive at a final budget number for the overall tactic.

Your tactics list finalized

Once you've established the budget number for a tactic, enter it into the tactics list to complete the details for this tactic. Now, your tactics list should look something like this:

Tactics List			
Tactic	**Launch Date**	**Who**	**How Much**
Develop Open House	6/1/02	Jay	$5,000

Follow this process for all other tactics in your plan, entering all data into your tactics list.

Maintenance and new tactics

If you're developing this tactics list, remember one thing. *Existing* marketing programs require time too—maintenance time. If your company currently has ongoing marketing campaigns, you must remember to build time into your marketing effort (and tactics lists) to keep these events moving ahead. All too often I see companies generate a healthy list of new tactics, all the while forgetting that their existing tactics require care and feeding too.

I learned this the hard way when I was marketing director for a national mattress manufacturer. When I came on board with the company, it already had underway a huge print advertising effort and a large-scale direct mail campaign. From there we expanded into radio and television advertising, along with new store openings across the US. As exciting as these new ventures were, they pulled my staff and me in too many directions, so much so that we started missing deadlines and simply didn't have time to think strategically any longer.

If we'd better recognized the time required for the maintenance of current marketing efforts, perhaps we could have managed the workload better.

Remember...

When you get to identifying your tactics, the end is in sight. This is one of the last steps in developing your marketing plan. Pay attention to the nitty-gritty's here and your marketing campaigns will go off that much smoother down the road.

Tools To Go

○ Tactics flow from your strategies.
○ First, brainstorm all possible tactics, then prioritize using the A-B-C method (page 120).
○ Flesh out the nitty-gritty's for your highest priority tactics.
○ Record key details for each tactic in your Tactics List.
○ Don't forget to account for maintenance tasks when allocating time for tactics.

"Unless structure
follows strategy,
inefficiency results."

Alfred Chandler,
Historian

Chapter 11

Timelines & Budgets: Two Powerful Controllers For Your Marketing

Now, I'd like to introduce you to two of the most powerful marketing tools available. One—the marketing timeline—helps organize your *time*, while the other—the marketing budget—helps organize your *money*.

Used together, the two furnish you with a powerful 1-2 combination to control and track your marketing efforts.

1. Marketing Timelines

What is a marketing timeline?

Back in the last chapter you developed a tactics list, lining out all your tactics and their launch dates. The marketing timeline takes this tactics list and supercharges it by lining out all *intermediate tasks* needed to complete each tactic. The result is a planning device so powerful it helps drive your weekly, daily, even hourly actions.

How to read a timeline

In this section, I've included a sample marketing timeline. See figure 1. Take a moment to study it and you'll notice that it's really a detailed, half-year-at-a-glance calendar. Across the column headings are the months in the year, and directly underneath each month appears a series of boxes with numbers. Each numbered box represents a week with the number in the box being Monday's date for that week. For example the "7" box underneath the month of January represents the week of January 7th.

Down the left-hand side of the page are blank row headings. On the first row I've listed a sample tactic called "Direct Mail Program", with 6 X's

Figure 1:   *'02 Timeline – 1st half of year only*

		Jan					Feb			
Program (leader)	**31**	**7**	**14**	**21**	**28**	**4**	**11**	**18**	**25**
Direct Mail program (Jay)			x	x	x	x	x	x	

directly across from it. The first X appears in the box directly underneath January 14, and the boxes continue through February 11, ending with the shaded box on February 18. These Xs account for your Direct Mail Program by telling you:

- Development begins the week of January 14
- It will take 6 weeks to develop <u>and</u>
- The program launches the week of February 18.

March				April					May				June			
4	11	18	25	1	8	15	22	29	6	13	20	27	3	10	17	24
									X	X	X	X	X	X		

If you look further to your right you'll see another set of boxes that represents your second direct mail campaign later that spring (May 6-June 10).

With the information listed in this manner, you now have a visual life for the tactic. A simple glance at the timeline tells you you're going to run your Direct Mail program twice, and lines out the start dates, duration and launch dates for both of these.

Not impressed yet? OK, imagine your timeline now includes *all* your annual tactics *and* their tasks. Now, your timeline might look like this:

Figure 2: *Emerge Marketing Annual Marketing Timeline –*

Program (leader)	Jan					Feb				March				April					May			
	1	8	15	22	29	5	12	19	26	5	12	19	26	2	9	16	23	30	7	14	21	28
New Product Launch (Jay)																						
Sales Collateral		S⇨C																				
Broadcast Fax				S⇨C																		
Broadcast Email						S⇨C																
Press Releases											S⇨C				S⇨C				S⇨C			
Press Release mail to lists												S⇨C				S⇨C				S⇨		
Brochure		S ⟹ C																				
Call Campaign											S ⟹ C											
Postcard-Marketing Report																S⇨C						
Postcard-Marketing Analysis																					S⇨C	

KEY: S=Start; C=Complete

Flushing out a tactic

Although at first glance this timeline may appear confusing, it's really a comprehensive planning tool that can visually represent your annual marketing plan, detailed step by step.

As you study this timeline, you can now begin to ask more strategic questions like:

- *When have we scheduled the majority of our marketing programs?*
- *Do we have a balanced marketing attack?*
- *How does our marketing sync up with the seasonality of our business?*
- *Do we have obvious voids where we won't be running marketing programs?*

Includes all programs 2001

June				July					Aug				Sept				Oct					Nov				Dec				
4	11	18	25	2	9	16	23	30	6	13	20	27	3	10	17	24	1	8	15	22	29	5	12	19	26	3	10	17	24	31

(Timeline chart with the following markers: S ⇨ C near Dec 17; S ⇨ C near Sept 15; S ⇨ C near Aug 20; C at June 4; S ⇨ C near Nov 19; S ⟹ C spanning Sept 10 to Oct 8.)

- *When will certain project leaders be busiest?*
- *Which tactics should I be working on the week of April 30?*

The timeline as a communication device

I've been in company-wide marketing meetings where this timeline was the only handout needed. Using it alone, the marketer could brief the rest of the attendees on the state of the company's marketing activities, and elicit their feedback.

And you'll be amazed how this tool opens up communications across departments. For example, if you're briefing the team on February's direct mail program, other departments can glance at the tactic's timeline and begin planning their support activities around it. The Telemarketing Department may realize it needs scripts ready by the week of February 18. The Finance Department needs to load the new pricing the week of February 11. Production can see they have to order additional raw materials the week of January 14 in order to get them in-house in time for production supporting the campaign.

Do you see what's happening? The timeline is driving the company, or more accurately the individuals in the company, to visualize their roles and responsibilities in supporting the marketing effort.

If you'd like a free timeline template for either 2002 or 2003, visit www.emergemarketing.com/publications.

The timeline as a management device

Furthermore, if you're a marketing manager with subordinates, you'll find the timeline to be an invaluable management tool. You can use it to monitor your staff's overall progress against key deadlines, or to identify resource bottlenecks you might face, and then plan actions to address them.

At a glance, you'll know what everyone (or in a smaller company, just you) should be working on at any point in time. Armed with this information you can more proactively identify your staff's (or your own) workload.

When you incorporate this timeline into your marketing effort, I'd suggest meeting with your subordinates, or other department heads, every 3 weeks to go over the timeline item by item.

Hang it up in front of your nose

Another way to maximize the usefulness of this tool is to hang it up. Don't just file it away in a folder, where you'll surely forget about it. Instead, make a copy and tape it up where your eye will see it every day. Maybe this is over your phone, or on your computer, or even on your cubicle wall. With the timeline in plain view, you'll be far more apt to see it and act upon its valuable contents.

Carry it around with you

Also, if you use a paper-based day planning system, shrink the timeline down and place a copy in your planner. I used to do this as a marketing director, and found it kept key marketing dates right at my fingertips. So, even if I was 3 time zones away and the controller asked me about the marketing effort for the second quarter, I had the details right in front of me. You'll never again say, "I'll have to get back to you with that information."

2. Marketing Budgets

Another powerful tool in your marketing effort is the marketing budget. Developed and maintained correctly, budgets provide you with financial data that can help manage your expenses and cash flow.

What budgets should look like

In Figure 3, you have an annual marketing budget for a fictitious company. In it, each tactic is a line item appearing on the left-hand side of the model.

Expenses appear across the row in the months you expect to pay the invoices. Notice that I said the *month you expect to pay the invoices—* not when the program runs. Very often there's a lag time between the two.

How to develop a budget

In the previous chapter, you developed a tactics list of all tactics and their total budget numbers. To develop your budgets, use a spreadsheet program and list all the tactics from your list on the rows to the left-hand side of the model.

Then, take the total budget numbers you've arrived at for each tactic and spread them into the appropriate months.

For example, if you budgeted $5,000 for two Trade Shows, one in March and one in September, you'd plug $2,500 into April and $2,500 into October. One half the expense—for the March show—would be paid in April, and the other half—for the September show—would be paid in October.

Figure 3:

Annual Budget for Biner Corporation (fictitious)

Category	Jan	Feb	March	April
Print Media	62,440	56,485	42,179	36,994
Broadcast/Outdoor Media	6,000	8,000	8,000	4,000
Yellow Pages	1,000	1,000	1,000	1,000
Publicity & Consumer Events			22,500	11,250
Internet				
Publicity	715	715	715	715
Graphic Services/Photo CD's	2,000	1,000		
Database Services	625	625	625	625
Brand Identity				
Direct Mail	3,250			3,250
Tie-In	1,667	1,667	1,667	1,667
Marketing Research			500	
Training	600	600		
Agent Self Promotion				715
Net Costs	**78,292**	**70,092**	**77,186**	**60,216**
Other Items				
Training & Education	250		250	
FAM Trips			1,000	
Promotions	500	500	500	500
Capital Improvements			1,500	
Opportunity Fund	1,547	1,351	3,174	1,835
Grand Total	**80,574**	**71,943**	**83,610**	**62,551**

If you're interested in downloading a free template for your own marketing budget, go to www.emerge marketing.com/publications

May	June	July	Aug	Sept	Oct	Nov	Dec	Total
23,669	35,812	25,130	21,773	34,094	40,970	37,532	34,471	451,549
					6,000	8,000		40,000
1,000	1,000	1,000	1,000	1,000	1,000	1,000	1,000	12,000
					11,250	11,250		56,250
	2,000	2,000	2,000	2,000	666	666	668	10,000
					715	715	710	5,000
								3,000
625					625	625	625	5,000
								0
	2,333	2,333	2,333		3,250	3,251		20,000
1,667	1,667	1,667	1,667	1,667	1,667	1,667	1,663	20,000
	500			500			500	2,000
								1,200
715	715	715	715	715	715			5,005
27,676	**44,027**	**32,845**	**29,488**	**39,976**	**66,858**	**64,706**	**39,637**	**631,004**
250		250		250		250		1,500
	1,000			1,000			1,000	4,000
500	500	500	500	500	500	500	500	6,000
	1,500			1,500			1,500	6,000
401	705	655	655	588	2,225	2,230	517	15,883
28,827	**47,732**	**34,250**	**30,643**	**43,804**	**69,583**	**67,686**	**43,154**	**664,387**

Build in "wiggle room" for each tactic

When I buy a pair of jeans, I buy them with a little extra "wiggle room". That way, if I make a mistake and overindulge at the buffet line, I can absorb the excess.

This same "wiggle room" principle should be used with your marketing budgets. How can you possibly anticipate everything that might happen with your marketing costs, over the course of a year, when putting together your budgets? You can't. So, you add in a little "wiggle room" in case:

• You underestimate the overall costs of a tactic.
• You experience cost overruns.
• Unexpected price increases occur while implementing a tactic (e.g. a postage increase).
• You must change vendors in the midst of a program—thus incurring additional set up charges.

In addition, with "wiggle room" in your budgets, you'll have some extra funds to "give back" to management in case your company faces an unexpected sales or profit shortfall. You can "find" money in your budget, cough it up and still not make an appreciable dent in your marketing programs.

So, after I've finished developing each tactic's budget number, I'll add 15% to it. This becomes my wiggle room.

Build in an opportunity fund

After costing out all your expected programs (you've included wiggle room, right?), add another item to your budget called *Opportunity Fund*. This is a lump sum amount that you'll plug in for new, and as yet unforeseen, opportunities.

Without this Opportunity Fund in your budget, you'll be forced to borrow money from other programs when some great new opportunity comes along. Maybe you can suddenly buy advertising in a strong publication at a severly reduced rate. Or, maybe you're contacted by a complimentary vendor, wanting to run a tie-in promotion with you. Whatever the opportunity is, your Opportunity Fund provides you with the flexibility to pursue it without detriment to your other programs.

How much should this fund be for? I typically devote 10% of a total marketing budget towards an opportunity fund (e.g. if your marketing budget is $50,000, your opportunity fund would be $5,000). But, if you decide to budget less, that's fine. Just squirrel away some money for those golden opportunities that are sure to come your way.

How much should you spend on marketing?

This is one of the most common questions I'm asked and the answer, as with so many things, is it depends. It depends on:

• *Your industry.* Some industries invest more on marketing than others (video games and cereal come to mind). Learn what companies in your industry are spending on their marketing. Consult industry publications, trade associations, and contacts you have in the industry to root out more details.

• *Your competitors' spending.* This information will be harder to come by but, it can still be found. Conversations with those who used to work for competitors may yield information. Also, official company documents, such as annual reports, might produce additional data. Other sources of potential information might include industry surveys or speeches given by company representatives.

Don't forget that astute observation, a calculator and a little creativity will go a long way towards producing some usable data. For example, answers to "How many times did they advertise in XYZ Publication?" and "How much does one insertion cost?", might go a long way towards an educated guesstimate of a competitor's advertising expenses.

• *What development stage your company is in.* If your company is just starting out, expect to spend a higher percentage of gross revenues on marketing. That's because you're busy building awareness for your company and generating trial for your products and services.

A more established business, with stronger industry awareness and word-of-mouth, will usually spend less on marketing.

• *How profitable your company is.* Let's face it, profitability is the ultimate score in the business world. And those companies with higher profit margins (like video games and cereal again) can allocate a higher percentage of funds towards marketing.

If your business is currently *un*profitable though, you have bigger fish to fry. Get profitable first, then and only then, should you spend this kind of time determining your marketing spending amount.

The most common range for marketing spending

Most small and midsized companies we deal with spend between *1%-10% of gross revenues* on marketing. I realize this is a large range, but at least it gives you a starting point.

Or, you could multiply your company's last year revenues by 1%, 5% and 10% and examine each of the numbers. Which of these can you afford? How do these numbers (or percentages) compare with your industry and competitors? The number or percentage that answers each of these questions best will be your marketing expense number for year one. And remember, you can always adjust the number next year.

Remember...

Remember the words of Sir Francis Galton, a scientist and explorer in the 19th century who said:

"Whenever you can, count."

Use timelines and budgets to help "count" your marketing effort.

Tools To Go

○ Consider using timelines for your marketing campaigns. Once you get the hang of them, you'll find them invaluable.

○ Every marketing effort should have a budget.

○ Build wiggle room and an opportunity fund into your budget.

○ Plan on investing 1-10% of your total revenues on marketing. Then, take a close look at industry and competitive spending patterns, what stage of development your company is in and its profitability to arrive at the right number.

"There are always
two creations:
the mental and
the physical.
The physical
creation always
follows the mental
creation."

Steven Covey,
Author

Chapter 12

Keys To Successfully Implementing Your Marketing Projects

Keep in mind that *developing* a marketing plan—and with it the countless hours of thinking, debating, squabbling, rethinking, consensus-building and finally committing it to paper—is only half the battle. In fact, all those valiant efforts are of little use if your marketing plan sits on a shelf collecting dust.

If you don't implement your marketing plan, your business could suffer for several reasons:

- You'll lose any momentum you've built to this point.
- You'll turn against you those who've willingly sacrificed their time to help you develop the plan.
- You'll forgo capitalizing on the greatest marketing vehicle of all time— the market itself.

Implementation hinges on the implementer

In most instances, *who* does the implementing is just as important as *what* gets implemented. That's because without the right captain at the helm of your marketing projects, you'll end up with a poorly implemented effort doing more damage to a company's image than no marketing at all.

One of the most important decisions you'll make in your marketing effort is *who* rolls it out. Don't short-change this decision. First, determine all the possible candidates in your company who could act in this role.

In smaller businesses, there may be only one candidate; the owner or the person responsible for marketing. But, in larger companies, you'll have a wider field to choose from. Consider lower level marketing members, other staff members with an interest in marketing, or administrative personnel before making your final decision.

Remember that marketing programs actually portray your company out into the marketplace. They can impress customers, prospects, suppliers, board members, investors, the media and even your competitors. With the right person leading your implementation charge, you'll put your best foot forward in the ultimate people's court—the market.

What makes for a great implementer?

The best marketing implementers possess a truly unique blend of talents—far different than the talents found in other departments. What does this person look like? Start with a dose of project manager, add in some accountant, throw in a dash of sales person, stir in a pinch of chemistry professor, sprinkle with a touch of high-wire acrobat, add a twist of ice-in-your-veins commodities broker, then top it all off with some lounge entertainer—and you have the right recipe!

The top qualities you'll find in all successful marketing implementers are:

• An upbeat attitude

To successfully roll out marketing campaigns, you need someone with a gleam in their eye. That's because rolling out marketing projects is a daunting task.

Any marketing effort, especially a brand new one, faces a host of obstacles. But the successful implementer, armed with an air of optimism, confronts them all safe with the knowledge that they can and will be completed.

These obstacles will usually come at the very worst time, but the upbeat marketer takes them all in stride.

• Initiative

As your implementer faces these obstacles (e.g. "we ran out of the paper-stock you wanted", "the vendor you chose has folded", "our database was accidentally deleted") this person will draw on his ability to creatively solve problems along the way. This is especially important in growing companies because the buck stops with this person. There simply isn't anyone else to delegate to. When it starts getting hot in the kitchen, you'll be glad you chose a marketing leader who exhibits initiative and requires only a minimum of hands on management.

• Plate-spinning skills

When I was a child, I watched *The Ed Sullivan Show* on television. On most episodes of this weekly variety show, Ed Sullivan would feature a "plate spinner" as a guest. Remember him? He'd start a plate spinning and place it on the top of a 3-foot dowel rod. Once that plate was smoothly spinning, he'd spin another plate to life on yet another dowel rod. After about a minute, the spinner would have 10 to 15 plates spinning simultaneously.

But where it got really interesting was when one of the first plates started losing its momentum and began wobbling. Everybody in the audience held their breath, expecting the plate to come crashing down. But just in the nick of time the plate spinner, with a flick of his wrist, would start the plate spinning again.

And right after spinning that plate back to life, another plate would start to wobble. And so on it went. *The marketing implementer is really a plate spinner.* She'll have to keep several (sometimes many) plates spinning all at once; each plate with its own momentum. Occasionally, she'll have to flick a project to life in order to keep its momentum.

To keep track of all these projects, notice when they're wobbling and inject momentum into them at just the right time requires good organizational skills.

• Get-along skills

As a marketer you'll work with the broadest array of people; more so than other functional departments. From vendors to customers, from accountants to sales reps, and from administrative staff to executives, a marketer interacts with a variety of personalities—sometimes all within the same hour. Your company's marketer should possess a flexible personality with good get-along skills.

The #1 mistake I see when hiring marketers

When I meet the marketing staff at a new client, I always ask about their background. Invariably, I learn that the person responsible for implementing marketing projects was hired because of her graphic design background. She was brought in to work on designing a new ad. After finishing that, she developed a new marketing brochure. About this time, the sales manager started complaining to her about the lack of a distributor in the East Coast. The following week, the finance director wondered aloud why product margins were falling. A week after that, the IT department approached her about launching an e-commerce website. Meanwhile, a key competitor was stealing market share with a new product—and the R&D staff wondered aloud to her why they hadn't launched their own new product. Everyone seemed to ask, all at the same time, "What is marketing going to do?" Poor designer!

What started as the ideal marketing design job for her (designing ads, creating brochures) had morphed overnight into a *real* marketing job— complete with issues of promotional mix, pricing, new product development and distribution.

Even if you have a raft of new ads or brochures that rest in your to-do pile, resist the temptation—with every bone in your body—to hire a graphic designer first. Instead, hire someone with a marketing background and a proven ability to manage projects. Graphic designers like to *design* things, not manage projects. And project management is one of the most valuable skills your marketing department needs to grow in the future.

Project management is the grounding

If you talked to a professional writer, you'd probably learn he spent thousands of hours writing short stories. If you talked to a professional football player you'd find he spent countless hours on the practice field working on his blocking and tackling. A leading speaker would have spent thousands of hours crafting his presentation skills. Every art has it's grounding and marketing's grounding is *project management*. Because so much of marketing is managing projects (even developing a marketing plan is a project), the really good marketers boast years of experience managing them. When you start looking at resumes for that inevitable marketing opening, ask yourself these questions:

- *What projects has this person managed from start to finish?*
- *Did they manage numerous projects concurrently?*
- *Was this person the project leader for these projects, or just a team member?*

A marketer without project management experience will soon be like a fish out of water when the serious marketing work gets underway. Stick to marketers with a solid grounding in project management.

5 keys to successful marketing implementation

Ok, let's say you've just finished your marketing plan—and then it hits you. How are you going to get all these marketing things done? Here are 5 things you *must* do to begin successfully implementing your marketing projects.

1 Wallow in the details

When you plan, you focus on the big picture. But when you execute, you shift perspectives. Instead of focusing on *why* something gets done, you now have to focus on *how* it gets done.

Always, on a daily basis, and for all active projects, ask yourself these questions:

○ What is the next step in this project?
○ Who is responsible for getting it done?
○ When will it be done by?
○ How are costs running on the project?

If you don't know the answers to these questions—go find them out immediately. One key to good project management is anticipation. And the more information you have at your fingertips, the better you can anticipate things.

2 Use a day planning system

To help you manage the myriad details of your projects, use some sort of day planning system. Whether it's paper-based or electronic is up to you. Whether it's this brand or that, again it's up to you. But without this very basic marketing tool, your implementation efforts will be doomed from the start. I found this out when I was a marketing assistant on a product with a $60 million marketing budget. Pretty soon, my to-do list covered 3 full pages, single-spaced. And things were falling through the cracks—big things! In short, my planning tools weren't sophisticated enough to tackle the tasks at hand.

Luckily though, I enrolled in a FranklinCovey® seminar that taught me the basics of time management and gave me the most valuable planning tool I've found—a Franklin Day Planner®. To this day, I still use it. If you're interested in learning more about this great marketing tool, visit www.franklincovey.com.

Don't wait until you're snowed under to make the same mistake. Employ a day planning system and take the time to understand how it works best for you. With this as a tool in your marketing toolkit, you'll find your marketing abilities will improve exponentially.

3 Plan for contingencies

Some believe it's pessimistic to ask, "What could go wrong?" Not me. When you ask that question, you put people through the process of visualizing possible mistakes—and fixes.

When a pilot draws up a flight plan, he also identifies alternate airports along the route. Then, if facing an emergency, he can divert to the alternate airport and seek safety. Is this pessimism? No, it's a realistic recognition that things can go wrong.

As a marketer, try to identify contingencies and corrective actions you can take before you need them. That way, you'll be far up the learning curve if something goes wrong.

4 Have regular project meetings

When I was Marketing Director in my corporate career, I insisted on project meetings every 2 weeks. During these meetings, the staff would update each other (and me) on all project status. These meetings are important for communication's sake.

But the *preparation* that occurs *before* these meetings is the real payoff. No one wants to look stupid in front of his or her peers, or boss. So, they'll check, recheck and triple-check deadlines, pricing, and responsibilities before the meeting.

Remember, marketing is the ultimate team game. Be sure you "huddle up" every so often. And make a habit of ending every meeting with the question "What are the next steps?" Then, don't leave the table until you have established what they are, when they'll be achieved, and by whom.

5 Honor deadlines

I'm a stickler on this for several reasons. First, when you develop a marketing plan, your deadlines reflect strategic details of your business (e.g. customer buying patterns, supply logistics). So when you miss a deadline, you're watering down the strategy behind that deadline.

More important, missing deadlines damages your credibility. Credibility with your boss, with your board, with your investors, and even with your fellow workers suffers if you consistently miss deadlines.

Finally, missing deadlines also allows complacency to creep into your operations. Miss enough deadlines, and no one takes them seriously. And if you're missing all your deadlines, move to the Bahamas; they don't care about deadlines either.

How to Better Manage Deadlines

• First, establish the drop dead

The most important deadline you'll manage to is called the *drop dead date*. This is the absolute, last date you, or anyone in your company, can "touch" a marketing vehicle (i.e. the final layout for a brochure, the proof on a direct mail piece, the final copy for your website). After this date, others outside your company will perform all remaining work on the project (i.e. printers, website developers, etc.).

Memorize this drop dead date, then don't tell anyone about it. This is an internal management fact that only *you* need to know.

• Now, manage to 5 days before the drop-dead date

After you've established your drop-dead date, establish another date *5 business days before it*. This is your "published deadline" and should be communicated to anyone who needs *to know it*.

You establish this second deadline because, as you'll find, no one respects your deadlines with the same sense of urgency as you. So, if you require management approvals on marketing copy, or you want to show someone in your office the proof, you'd then give him the published deadline as the time you need his action by.

That way, if things get off track or you run into an unplanned incident (death in the family, sudden illness) you've got yourself covered and can still keep the project on-track. And on the bright side, if your published date is met, then you'll be that much farther ahead on the project.

• Don't forget about maintenance tasks

I mentioned this in a previous chapter, but it bears repeating. If your marketing effort is more than a year old, you'll probably have maintenance tasks to budget for—both mentally and financially. Any program you're repeating, or any ongoing marketing task (e.g. issuing marketing reports, reviewing P&L's, generating forecasts) should be accounted for in your timelines and budgets.

• 10% Better

I'd like to issue you a challenge. This summer, resolve to mow your lawn 10% better—each time. So next week, mow the lawn and edge it. The following week, mow and then plant some grass seed. The week after that, mow and aerate the lawn. Can you imagine how nice your lawn would look after a summer of that?

Now, apply that principle to your marketing effort. Got an internal newsletter? Or an ongoing direct mail campaign? How about a series of newspaper ads? Routine website maintenance?

Each time one of these projects begins, resolve to make it 10% better than the last time. I use this principle with all our clients and you know what? Not only do the pieces look nicer, but the phones ring more.

• Copy yourself on all marketing campaigns

If you want to experience your company's marketing the way your customers do, add your name to your own mailing list. That way, you'll receive your company's marketing messages exactly the same way your customers do.

Furthermore, if you're like most marketers who develop marketing campaigns, you can get too close to a campaign to remain truly objective about it. I find it's very hard amidst the mundane chores of proofreading, color checking and quality control when developing a new marketing piece, to keep the overall objective in mind. You're so busy looking at the bark, you can't see the forest.

By receiving your company's marketing communications, just as your customers would (in the mail, via email, etc.) you'll be forced to step back and assess the piece from your customers' vantage point.

I remember one instance where our company designed some teaser copy for the outer envelope of a client's direct mail piece. It looked fine to us as it went to press. However, when I received my copy of the direct mail package at home, I saw much to my chagrin, that the post office had applied a barcode sticker *right* over the teaser copy. You couldn't even read it. Disappointing yes, but because I included my name on the mailing list, I learned a valuable lesson that day (all teaser copy must appear at least 5/8" above the bottom of a direct mail piece) and have never repeated it.

• Tackle a task a day

At the very basis of marketing implementation is <u>momentum</u>. This is a key word in your quest for marketing success. To get and keep marketing momentum, your marketing effort must be continuous and sustained.

Successful marketing campaigns don't take the summer off, nor are they created by working on them "when I have the time." You must make the time. If your problem is finding time in the day to work on marketing, just remember this saying:

A task a day, keeps your marketing in play[©].

Make a mental promise to accomplish one marketing task a day. It doesn't have to be a huge task. Maybe it's phoning a supplier to get a quote, or meeting with the sales manager to get ideas for a new brochure. Whatever the task, the simple act of accomplishing it will fill you with confidence and momentum.

• Eliminate one marketing task each year

I can't count the number of stressed out marketers I've seen over the last 15 years. As task after task is added to their plates (the test launch in Albuquerque, new packaging for the Gizmo line, new database query software, a new set of budget reports), nothing is ever removed. In short, this is a prescription for burnout.

Stop this madness at once, and identify one task each year you can eliminate. Then, jettison it. All too often, someone gets used to doing something repeatedly (e.g. issuing a department report, attending certain staff meetings), yet the task isn't creating value for the business.

What everyone's forgotten is that somebody (read <u>YOU</u>) sinks boatloads of time into these tasks, without any benefit. So, I advise our clients to look hard for one marketing task they can eliminate in the year ahead. Your health and sanity depend on it.

• Consider going outside

You could probably do your own plumbing or hang your own drywall, but is that really the best use of your time? If marketing isn't your passion or ability, outsource it. The peace-of-mind *you* get and the momentum *your business* gets will be well worth the investment.

Remember...

When I think of marketing implementation, I think of my baseball coach's advice:

"Put the ball in play.
Get runners on base.
Move them around.
Work on your fundamentals."

Words that are quite apropos to the field of marketing implementation.

Tools To Go

- ○ Great marketers possess initiative, an upbeat attitude, organizational skills and the ability to get-along with people.

- ○ Don't make the #1 mistake in hiring marketers—instead, hire project managers.

- ○ Project management is the "blocking and tackling" of marketing.

- ○ Establish drop dead dates and published deadlines for all projects.

- ○ Copy yourself on all campaigns.

- ○ Tackle a task a day.

- ○ Eliminate one each year.

"In the long run,
men hit only what
they aim at."

Henry David Thoreau,
Author

Chapter 13

Marketing Metrics: Keeping Your Finger on the Pulse

Recently, I visited a friend who was recuperating in the hospital. As I sat by her bedside, a steady stream of nurses drifted in to take her temperature, read her charts, monitor her blood pressure, and check her medicine schedules. After a nurse had taken new temperature and blood pressure readings from the patient, she diligently recorded these values into a computer monitor that stood off to one side.

After entering the values into the computer, the nurse studied the historical data points, already in the computer, that represented the patient's vitals over the last 24 hours. The nurse would then inform the patient that her blood pressure was dropping or her temperature was moderating.

Shortly after, a doctor would troop in. After making small talk with the patient, he would head straight for the computer where the historical data points were stored. From this data, he could then familiarize himself with the patient's progress over the course of the last day. Occasionally, after reviewing the computer data, the doctor would recommend to the nurse a change in the medicine schedule or a modification to her rehabilitation schedule. *And then it hit me.*

This is the same process successful marketers use when evaluating their marketing programs. They monitor, record and analyze valuable data, much the same way the nurses and doctors did. Then, from these historical measurements, or *metrics*, marketers can make changes in strategy or tactics.

What's that you say? You *don't* measure your marketing efforts? Then, let's back up for a second and re-imagine the hospital scene. Only this time, pretend the nurse didn't take any measurements. Instead of monitoring the patient's temperature and blood pressure, the nurse made the beds and checked the room temperature.

In this new scenario, the doctor arrives yet doesn't have any data, charts, or a computer monitor to review. He asks the nurse how the patient is doing, but this time the nurse replies "I don't know. She looks better, but I have no way of knowing."

Sadly, this is how most marketing efforts are measured and tracked today. No one captures measurements for the effort and so no one knows how the effort is progressing. There aren't any metrics, reports, and quantitative discussions—in short, everyone's in the dark. Predictably, when I ask most companies how their marketing effort is going, everyone sheepishly looks at their shoes, shrugs and answers "We don't know." I get the feeling that deep down they know they should track their metrics, but for whatever reason, they don't.

This chapter is designed to give you a basic understanding of marketing metrics and provide you with several you can start using today.

What metrics do for you

The metrics you use don't have to be complicated, just revealing. Every statistic that you spend valuable time compiling should act as a window into your marketing effort. Each metric should tell you something significant about your effort. Otherwise, what's the point?

One benefit to using marketing metrics is that they alter the way you think. Using metrics, you'll start thinking in a more disciplined fashion, by asking more detailed and strategic questions that follow a logical train of thought. And the answers you gain will spur you on, in turn, to expect greater things from your marketing.

For example, after analyzing your lead generation efforts, you may find your company getting lots of leads, yet not closing many of them into sales. Is that because your prices are too high? Could it be because you lack a money-back guarantee? Is there a significant difference between your product and competitors' that prospects find out only after contacting you? As you address these more strategic questions head-on, you'll quite likely uncover a deeper, more strategic problem that must be fixed. It's at this point that you go from treating symptoms to treating the real illness.

I tell all our clients that one important goal is to banish forever the response "I don't know" when asked how your marketing is coming along.

Marketing metrics fall into two broad classes:

- Basic health metrics and
- Efficiency metrics

Let's take them one at a time.

Basic marketing health metrics

The first set of metrics concern themselves with the overall health of your marketing efforts. Since these metrics focus more on the big picture view of your marketing effort, and are used as first-glance diagnostics, consider them the equivalent of taking your marketing's pulse.

From these metrics, you'll formulate preliminary judgements about your efforts and identify areas for further observation.

Here are just a few of the more common *health metrics*:

• New Inquiries

Inquiries (or leads) for a company are its lifeblood. These inquiries turn into prospects, which in turn convert into customers, who then generate referrals. As your business grows, you'll find your new business development efforts will crave new leads like a fire craves oxygen.

You'll soon find that having meaningful metrics in place helps you:

○ Assess the overall health of your marketing effort.

○ Identify trouble spots in your marketing.

○ Point out successful marketing activities that should be capitalized upon—maybe even expanded.

○ Identify to yourself and other stakeholders (i.e. employees, board members) that your marketing efforts are making progress and adding value to your company.

A few basic ways leads are generated:

○ Calling and requesting a brochure.
○ Leaving a card at your trade show booth.
○ Emailing you with a question.
○ Sending in a reply card.
○ Registering on your website.
○ Getting your name from someone else.

When someone approaches your company in any of these ways, it means you've generated their interest. Track the overall number of your company's inquiries on a *monthly* basis. By doing this, you'll begin to answer questions like:

• *What is the seasonality of our business?*
• *What is the average number of monthly leads we generate?*
• *Which programs generate the most leads for us?*

If you track this metric any less often than monthly, you might not give yourself adequate time to react to market developments. For example, if your business enjoys a strong winter seasonality (i.e. snowplowing, hot cereals), and you calculate your metrics quarterly, then more than half of your selling season will be over before you examine your metrics. And this leaves you precious little time to take corrective actions, if needed.

• Source of leads

Just as important as how many leads you get is where they come from. Each month that you report on total inquiries, you should also try to break down the origins of these leads. It might look something like this:

Lead Source Report–February

Source	#	%
Referrals	10	40
Direct Mail	7	28
Yellow pages	5	20
Website	3	12
TOTAL	**25**	**100**

From an analysis like this, taken across a few months time, you'll begin to single out those programs that produce the most responses, and those that don't.

• New Customer Sales

Old customers go away for several reasons. They switch to your competitors, they take their business in-house or they can just plain go out of business. Plan on this attrition—it's all too common in the business world. Therefore, your marketing should address this issue by seeking a steady stream of new customers to replace those you lose.

Define a new customer as one who has 24 months or less of revenue history with you, and then generate a quick report showing your new customers, ranked by sales—high to low, and where they came from.

It might look like this:

New Customer Sales Report

Customer	Annual Sales	Source
XYZ Inc.	$ 300,000	Yellow pages
ABC Co.	$ 240,000	Referral-Trade Assn.
Climb On Inc.	$ 174,000	Yellow pages
On Belay Inc.	$ 124,000	Referral-ABC Co.
Beasley's	$ 94,000	Direct Mail

Prepare this report every January for the preceding year & you may begin to notice a pattern around where new customers are coming from, and what attracts them to your doorstep. Using the example above, what preliminary conclusions could you draw?

• New Product Revenue

When I worked for a large consumer goods company, we religiously tracked new product revenue (revenue from products launched within the last 5 years). This was an important barometer because new products and services always intrigue consumers. At last count, largely fueled by new product proliferation, an average grocery store carries over 31,000 items! Whether or not this is right, we marketers have trained consumers to look for new products.

You could generate a report at the end of every year that broke down your sales by new and old product revenue.

• Profitability by project or customer

It's good to know your sales picture. It's even better to know your profit picture. Since profitability is a marketer's true barometer, we should watch it like a hawk.

If your business is project oriented (e.g. a consulting practice or an engineering firm) or you can easily separate out customer revenues, you may find it helpful to track your profitability by project or customer.

To do this, take all revenue for a project, then subtract all direct costs associated with the project. The remaining amount is your total project profit. Now as a second step, divide the total project profit by the total project revenue number and you'll arrive at a profit margin percentage. For example:

Profit Margin Calculation

Total project revenue	$7,500
Less total project costs	– $2,190
Equals Gross Profit	= $5,310 (gross profit)
Divided by total project revenue	÷ $7,500
Equals Gross margin	= 71% (gross margin)

After calculating this margin number for a variety of projects, you'll start to see that some projects (or clients) have higher profit margins than others. After doing this you may wonder:

• *Why are margins higher for some projects than others? Is it because of lower costs? Higher prices?*

• *Now knowing the margins for these projects, would we do them all again? If not, why?*

If you're a larger company, a good cost accounting system makes this job easier. But even if you're a smaller company, you can still arrive at these metrics with a little digging and a good calculator. Once you get in the habit of tracking these metrics, the results will be eye-opening and you'll make it a strategic priority for your business.

Efficiency Metrics

The other important set of metrics you'll use are *efficiency metrics*. These measures are used to evaluate the actual spending efficiencies behind your marketing efforts—that is to say how well your marketing money is being spent. From these metrics, you'll get a deeper analysis of your specific marketing programs. You'll start to learn which marketing efforts cost you the most, which cost you the least and, overall, which produce the biggest bang for your marketing buck. Among these measures are:

• Cost per inquiry (CPI)

Also called *cost per lead*, this is a simple metric that is extremely valuable in pointing out which marketing programs work hardest for you. When I worked for a direct marketing firm, we calculated CPI's for every single publication we advertised in (which was well over a hundred at one point), thus providing a wealth of knowledge about the performance for all our

---

Other health metrics you could use:

○ Sales calls per week

○ Presentations per week

○ Proposals per month

○ Average revenues per sales call

○ Number of lost customers

○ Percentage of sales sold off a promotion

○ Average price per sale

○ Sales per employee

○ Market share (that is, what % share of the overall market your business owns)

○ Close ratio (the % of inquiries you turn into orders)

advertising publications. From this analysis, we learned which were the most productive vehicles in our marketing, and which were not.

For measuring the pure efficiency and impact of your marketing spending, the CPI metric can't be beat.

Here's how you calculate it:

Cost per Inquiry Calculation

Total Marketing Expenses for a Program $2,500

Divided by Total Inquiries   ÷ 15

Equals Cost per Inquiry (CPI)   = $166

Total marketing expenses for a program could include any or all of these expenses:

- Graphic design
- Copywriting
- Printing
- Postage
- All trade show costs
- All website costs
- Media placement (e.g. ad space, banner ads)
- Pay for performance costs (e.g. pay-per-click)
- Costs for consultants
- Any other costs you incur in your marketing.

Now, if last year's cost per inquiry number was $250, then this year's figure of $166 means you're making headway because your costs of acquiring a lead are dropping. Conversely, if this year's figure is more than last years, your marketing is less efficient and you'll want to dig into it.

For companies with multiple product lines, or a wide variety of marketing programs, you may want to take this analysis one step further by calculating CPI's for each product line or marketing program.

• Cost per Order (CPO)

At the same time you're calculating CPI, you can also calculate your *cost per order*. This is calculated like this:

Cost per Order Calculation

Total Marketing Expenses for a Program $2,500

Divided by Total Orders   ÷ 5
Equals Cost per Order (CPO)   = $500

Whereas CPI is a measure of your spending efficiency to obtain inquiries, CPO measures your efficiency in closing orders. CPO is always higher than CPI because you'll always have more inquiries than orders. But if your CPO is significantly higher than your CPI (say, 10 or more times higher), that may indicate that your weakness is in converting inquiries into orders (i.e. your sales force needs training, you lack certain sales collateral).

How to calculate a program's breakeven

As you get more comfortable with metrics, you should start calculating *breakeven points* for each marketing program. The breakeven point is a number you calculate before a program runs, that identifies the actual number of orders you'll need to cover all program costs. Here's how you calculate it:

Breakeven Calculation

Total Marketing Expenses for a Program $2,950

Average Profit from a Sale $500
Divide Marketing Expenses by Average Profit $2,950 ÷ $500
Equals Breakeven Orders   = 5.9 or 6 orders

Knowing this measure will help you establish expectations for each program you run.

 Web Metrics

If you're like other companies these days, a website increasingly figures into your marketing mix. But what exactly is it doing for you? Use a web analytics package (e.g. www.superstats.com) to help answer that question.

Among the most valuable web metrics to track are:
1. Unique visitors per day.
2. Page views per day.
3. Average page views per visitor.
4. Most popular pages on the site.
5. Common search phrases used.
6. Most common site entry point.
7. Most common site exit point.
8. Most requested pages.
9. Top referring sites.
10. Busiest times of day for your site.

Establish targets for each marketing program

Once you start developing breakevens, it follows naturally that you'll develop targets, before your program is launched. For example, if you're planning for a trade show, in addition to developing a breakeven, you might want to set a target for new contacts made. If your expected show attendance is 3,000 people, you could set a goal of getting business cards from 10% or 300 of them.

You could also establish targets for:
• Number of orders written at the show or
• Number of demonstrations given.

Whatever target you set for your business, make sure it's attainable and realistic. Then communicate this target to everyone who'll have a hand in attaining it at the show. In the trade show example given above, I'd communicate your target (let's say it's the number of people registering at your booth) to everyone who'll be working the booth. That way, all clearly understand the expectation for the show and have more incentive in attaining it.

Realize the intangibles

It's time for a pop quiz:

- How can you measure your company's awareness among prospects?
- How do you measure the credibility you've created in new customer's minds?
- How would you track word-of-mouth mentions from a publicity campaign?

And the answer to all three is—you can't! Marketing is gray—not black and white, and these are all examples of qualitative benefits achieved. All are extremely valuable to your marketing effort—yet none can be tracked. Resign yourself to this fact—parts of your marketing can't ever be measured. Your Chief Financial Officer won't like it, but it's true.

Sure-fire ways to capture metrics

When I worked in sales for a computer software company, our ads suggested the reader call our toll-free 800 number and ask to speak to Sandy Hills. In reality, there wasn't anyone named Sandy Hills; we made her up as a way to tip off the receptionist to a new caller. Although I don't suggest this approach to everyone, it was a creative way to help capture our metrics. Whenever someone asked for Sandy Hills, the receptionist then recorded that as a new inquiry from our advertising. Other ways to help capture your metrics are:

- *Make it an ingrained habit to ask "How did you hear about us?"* This is far and away the best method, especially for smaller businesses. In addition to being a good icebreaker, it immediately helps the salesperson determine the quality of the lead.

- *Add a "Lead Source" box to your sales orders.* When the order paperwork is processed by the salesperson, he must write in a code identifying how the prospect came to him. Otherwise the order can't be processed.

• *Distribute preprinted notepads to your salesforce.* The sales person can check off any of various lead source options as she carries on a conversation with the prospect.

• *Add key codes to your promotional pieces.* We've all been asked by a catalog company to read the "key code found on the back cover." There's a reason. Once that code is put into the computer, it identifies the specific catalog the caller has in front of them, and spells out any special discounts they might be entitled to.

How do I record this lead?

More and more often, I find that prospects reference a variety of marketing vehicles when asked how they heard about a company. They say something like "Well, I'm on your mailing list, my friend loves buying your clothes and then I saw a billboard on my way home from work." What's the correct source for that lead—direct mail, billboards, or referral? If your system will allow, check all three. Each of these vehicles *did* play a part in getting them to call you. If your system doesn't allow for multiple entries, use the first one you hear.

Scorecards: The need for monitoring

To help you collect and report on your metrics, I recommend using a Marketing Scorecard. The scorecard example here is one we've used with our clients. Obviously your metrics reported on the scorecard may be different from these. But this is a handy format to report the data on. [See Figure 4.]

There are several benefits to using a Marketing Scorecard. First, it records all your marketing metrics in a standard format, so tracking historical changes is easier. Second, more strategic discussion occurs when you have all your numbers together on one report, side-by-side. Finally, presenting the metrics using a Marketing Scorecard further reinforces how important tracking metrics is to your marketing effort.

Remember...

Vow to eliminate the phrase "I don't know" when talking about your company's marketing performance. Make metrics a sturdy tool in your toolkit and you'll see better results follow.

Figure 4:

Readme Publications Scorecard
Period January '01

1. Revenue & Orders

	Monthly			YTD		
	2001	2000	% +/-	2001	2000	% +/-
Revenue						
Orders						

Rationale:

This is where your narrative would go. You'd plug in any discussion of the numbers here.

2. Marketing

	Monthly			YTD		
	2001	2000	% +/-	2001	2000	% +/-
Marketing Expenses						
Cost per Order (CPO)						

Rationale:

3. Sales

	Monthly			YTD		
	2001	2000	% +/-	2001	2000	% +/-
Outbound Calls						
Inbound Calls						

Rationale:

Tools To Go

○ Metrics help you keep a finger on the pulse of your marketing efforts.

○ Make use of both basic health metrics and efficiency metrics.

○ Realize that marketing results in some intangible benefits—those that are unmeasurable. You'll never be able to track them with metrics, but they're still vitally important.

"A good name is
more desirable then
great riches."

Proverbs 22:1

Chapter 14

The Keys to Branding Your Company

During the 19th and early 20th centuries, a rancher would mark his cattle with a unique brand. This brand, which depicted an image unique to his ranch, distinguished his cattle from another ranch's in the event of a broken fence.

Branding, in today's modern marketing world, operates much the same way. These days, branding is used to distinguish a product or service from a competitor's by establishing certain images in the prospect's mind. And in today's super-competitive market, it's a key marketing tool. Without it, your marketing effort as a whole rests not on a solid foundation, but rather on the shifting sands of a weak brand.

Branding the company

For most companies out there, brand elements are among the first things a prospect sees. Whether the prospect visits a website, peruses a brochure or stops by the company's trade show booth, the prospect walks away with impressions of the company's brand.

My advice to growing companies is to pay dear attention to your branding programs from the outset. Remember that one objective of your marketing program is to strengthen the "link of trust" between you and your prospect. Branding can be one of the most effective ways to do this.

Shaping your brand image

When developing a branding strategy, consider first the personality you want your brand to convey. Is it sexy or sweet? Tough or tender? Laid-back or cutthroat? These are just a few of the brand characteristics that go into a brand image. And if you think all this is hooey, play along with me for a moment and consider these questions: Do Marlboros really taste different than other cigarettes? Is AOL really better than Yahoo? Is H&R Block superior to the tax accountant down the street? No to all three!

These products are leaders because they're leading brands. The core product or service is of secondary importance to many consumers. Instead, people want to do business with a product they identify with and trust—and that gets back to the brand image.

What do you want your company's brand image to be? If you have trouble with that question, try equating your brand to a famous person. Do you want it to be John Wayne? Jimmy Stewart? George Clooney? Wesley Snipes? Sylvester Stallone?

Do you want it to be more like Helen Hayes? Audrey Hepburn? Madonna? Lil Kim? Shirley Temple? Choosing a celebrity can help you zero in on your brand's characteristics. For example, if you seek a brand personality that's sweet, kind and gentle, it's probably like Helen Hayes. If it's tough, strong and proud, it's probably John Wayne.

Once you've chosen a complimentary personality, try to identify those characteristics that made you associate your company's image with that person. Once identified, these characteristics will form the basis for your brand image.

Name: A crucial first step

How different would you be if your name was Clem or Matilda? A company or product name sets the tone for future marketing efforts. If the name is well crafted, your marketing messages carry much more impact.

Company or product names can be generated from invented words (Xerox), initials (IBM), founder's names (Johnson & Johnson), as well as several other methods. Make sure your name is distinctive, memorable, crafts the right image and can be protected.

According to the book *Crafting the Perfect Name* (Alder Press, 1995), the popularity of company name lengths, by number of words, is:

Two words:	9%
Three words	50%
Four words	35%
Five or more words	6%

A good name should:

○ Promote the desired image.

○ Communicate a benefit.

○ Be easy to read, spell and pronounce.

○ Be memorable.

○ Be protectable.

○ Provide room for growth (e.g. Aldrich Street Cleaners might be a problem if it ever moved away from Aldrich St.).

○ Be easy to find when listed in a directory or phone book (e.g. where do you look for 2 Close for Comfort?)

Ways of choosing a name

Here are some of the more common ways to develop a product or company name:

1. Benefit Oriented Names

Examples: U-Haul, Emerge Marketing

I most often recommend using a benefit orientation in your name. Whether it's a company name or product name, this approach singles out a key benefit you deliver to the consumer. Here are three examples of company names with benefit orientations: Sprint, UHaul and Budget Car Rental. It's not hard to envision what each brand purportedly stands for, is it? OK now here are three of their competitors: Eschelon, Koch National Lease and Americar. What do they stand for? Don't ask me, because I don't know.

The benefit approach to naming will establish in your prospects' mind faster *who* you are and *what* you do. Use it if you can.

2. Invented Names

Examples: Intel, Exxon, Compaq

These names don't actually mean anything. But they are easier to protect legally and I guess that explains their growing popularity. A name by this method will be distinctive, but how memorable will it be? And although one of these will be easier to protect legally, will it promote the desired image?

Like most things, this method is a trade-off, but just make sure your name is strong enough to overcome the inherent weaknesses in using this approach.

3. Combination Names

In *Crafting the Perfect Name*, the authors outline a simple process for generating a company name. First, they divide the name up into 3 sections; the *distinctive* part of the name **(Who)**, the *primary* activity of the company **(What)** and the *type of organization* **(How)**.

Then, they suggest brainstorming various word options for each section. Using a fictitious example, your naming options tool might look like this:

Figure 5:   *Naming Options Tool*

Distinctive Name (Who)	Activity (What)	Type of Organization (How)
Aldrich	Marketing	Company
Dunleavy	Research	Associates
Aplomb	Real Estate	Corporation
Keynote	Payroll Processing	International
Success	Software	Partners
Reach	Knowledge	Group

Now using this grid, you would choose the best word option in each section and combine those into a company name. In the example above, I've generated a few options—do any of them read better than others?

4. Founder's Names

Examples: Johnson & Johnson, Hewlett-Packard

Before I start here, remember that our business world is quite different than it was only 30 years ago. In those days, you could name your company Hewlett-Packard and stand a chance of breaking through the clutter. Today,

I don't think you can. These days there are just too many messages clamoring for people's attention. The name Hewlett Packard, standing on its own, doesn't help describe the business you're in, nor the benefits you provide. I generally don't recommend this approach.

There are a couple caveats to this. If you have a distinctive name, that is easy to pronounce and spell, then it might make sense. Also, if you're a famous personality with equity already built into your name (e.g. Henry Kissinger & Associates), then it makes sense. And in certain professions (legal & accounting come to mind) it's an established practice to use founder's names.

However, if you can come up with a good name using another method, I would.

5. Acronym and Lettered Names

Examples: IBM, ABC, FMC

This is my least favorite method to name a company. However, many companies use it and some have had to migrate to this approach. Either they acquired another company, their capabilities have expanded past their original name, or they've diversified their business (e.g. 3M is actually an abbreviation for Minnesota Mining and Manufacturing).

I don't generally recommend this naming approach. After all, it's not particularly memorable, distinctive or thought provoking. However, I do recommend this approach when most people in the market already use an abbreviated moniker to describe your company. For example, if your company, Industrial Plastics Corporation, is referred to as "IPC". Otherwise, take a pass on this alphabet-soup approach.

6. The dreaded "& Associates"

Examples: Too numerous to count

I meet with a lot of folks who are just launching a new company. They proudly take me through their business idea, and then slide a business card across the table. My heart sinks though when I read *Joe Blow & Associates*. Instead of working hard for a distinctive name, they've instead chosen the easy way, what I call the "ego-trip method".

I'll probably get a lot of people's noses out of joint by saying this but, naming your company after yourself is limiting. Furthermore, *and Associates* typically connotes you're new in business, and five years from now, if you have 10 employees, you'll still be communicating "new" to the market.

How to protect your name

Once you've decided on a name, how do you protect its use? There are a number of steps available to protect it, but which ones you take depend on these factors:

- The geographic scope of your business' physical assets
- Whether your Internet site conducts commerce
- Your type of business.

If your business is strictly local (e.g. Aldrich Street Cleaners), then you'd want to register the name with the Secretary of State's office in your state. You can usually call up the office and request a cursory search over the phone for the company name you want. Then, at their website (Minnesota's is www.sos.state.mn.us), you can download application forms. By filling these out, and submitting a fee (somewhere in the neighborhood of $25), you'll officially register your company name with the Secretary of State's office.

I'd also recommend publishing your company name quickly after you get confirmation back from the Secretary of State's office. This helps you gain visibility, but more importantly it establishes a permanent record of "first use" for the name. Immediately after receiving confirmation of my company name, I published an announcement declaring our business' formation in two consecutive issues of a local legal journal. This public record of first-use proved important 8 years later when our company was involved in a trademark dispute.

If your business is a corporation, many states require you to include words such as *corporation, company, incorporated* or *limited* in your name. Read the fine print closely when filling out the forms from the Secretary of State.

Doing business in other states

If your trading area will include other states, you'll probably want to register your name in them. You can do this by writing the Secretary of State's office in those states and requesting the forms. I'm told you can register in all 50 states through the mail.

Trademarks

According to the dictionary, a trademark is "any word, name, symbol or device, or any combination thereof used by a person, or which a person has a bona fide intention to use in commerce, to identify and distinguish his or her goods including a unique product from those manufactured or sold by others and to indicate the source of the goods, even if the source is unknown." Whew! Trademarks can be registered in individual states or at the federal level through the U.S. Patent and Trademark Office (USPTO). For more information, visit www.uspto.gov/

3 Reasons to seek a trademark

○ If you anticipate expanding into new markets, a trademark affords you protection to do this.

○ A trademark can pose one more barrier to entry for your competitors.

○ If battling competitors who are importing knock-off versions of your product is an issue, a trademark helps.

Please be advised that the trademark laws are complex, so if you're thinking of getting a trademark, consult with a trademark lawyer.

Logo: your company's symbol

A logo is a distinctive symbol that helps identify a company. The cost to develop a logo can run tens of thousands of dollars, or it can be free. For another business venture of mine, I discovered an image in a catalog of public domain logos. With some cutting and pasting, I developed it into a company logo...absolutely free.

If you're serious about a logo though, I recommend hiring a good design firm. The right logo goes a long way towards crafting an image for your company. Here are some guidelines to follow when developing a logo:

- It should communicate easily and not confuse.
- It should synch up with your positioning.
- It should be distinctive.
- It should be an enduring image—one that will last for years.

Once you've developed several concepts, I'd test each in color and black and white. I'd test them in a variety of sizes. I'd test them in a variety of locations on your materials. Once you select a logo that's effective and has withstood all these tests, you'll now possess a real marketing asset.

Taglines: A memorable definition

I'm a big believer in taglines. In 10 words or less a good tagline can plant in a prospect's mind, the core essence of a brand. And for smaller companies, it can be one of the most efficient marketing weapons in their arsenal.

A tagline is simply a short description of a business' reason for being. It can incorporate elements of its expertise, it's target audience, even the markets it serves. Taglines can be both direct and subtle—whatever it takes to get the prospect to say to themselves "Oh, I get it."

How can you develop a tagline for your business? There's a real art to it, but here's an exercise that might generate a working tagline:

Tagline Exercise

Fill in the blanks to these questions

1. Our expertise is in _____

_____

_____

_____

(which field?)

2. We offer our customers _____

_____

_____

_____

(your products or product category)

3. We appeal best to _____

_____

_____

_____

(your target audience)

So, let's say your answers were:
1) Payroll
2) Software products <u>and</u>
3) Time starved HR professionals

Now take your answers to these 3 questions and insert them into this sentence:

XYZ Company: _____   _____

for_____.

⇩

Then, your working tagline using this model would be:

XYZ Company: Payroll Software Products for Time Starved Professionals.

At this stage, I recommend taking take this working tagline to a copy-writer or marketing consultant. In a hour or two (if they're any good) they can make this tagline a bit more 'zingy'. What you're after is a memorable and pithy tagline, that summarizes your key reason for being.

Attach it to your logo

Once you have a tagline, always connect it to your logo as a standard prac-tice. Either place the tagline below your logo or alongside it. But, whenever your logo appears, your tagline should be with it. This further defines your image and gives the prospect two different ways to experience your company—through pictures and words.

Some people process information better through pictures, others through words. Linking your logo and tagline helps appeal to both sets of people and will make your brand clear as a bell.

Fonts and typestyles

Along with names, logos and taglines, fonts and typestyles help define your brand. Have your creative designer standardize your fonts so that you use just a few as company standards. Make sure they are easy to read and convey the image you want.

More importantly though, make sure these are readily available fonts. We once had a designer develop a brand using a font that was extremely difficult to find. So, when it came time to develop printed materials using this hard-to-find font, the printer didn't have it. We had to shell out several hundred dollars more just to purchase this font for our printer.

Marketing colors: The mood for your visual identity

How do you feel when you walk into a yellow room? When you see a sign with a red background color, what's your first reaction? If you see someone dressed all in black, what's the first thought in your mind? Colors generate emotional reactions, and it's important to carry that over into your branding program.

So, here is a quick list of common colors and the emotions behind them:

Color	Emotions behind the color
Red	Stop, energy, passion
Yellow	Caution, cowardice
Green	Go, safe, sexual arousal
White	Purity, virtue
Black	Luxury, prestige, evil
Blue	Authority, calm, masculinity
Orange	Strength, stimulation
Brown	Warmth, comfort
Purple	Royalty

Just as important is knowing which colors your competitors use—so you can avoid them. If you're trying to distinguish your brand from the competitors, choose a color (or color family) that your competitors do not use.

Get copies of color brochures or logos from all your competitors and see which colors they've staked out. Then, differentiate yourself through the use of a distinctive color.

If your company has an international presence, you'll want to know what stigmas are attached to your company color in the host country. For example, China views red as the most appealing color. Blue however, a very popular brand color in the U.S., is perceived in China as evil or sinister. If your company has international offices, consider how your color plays in these countries.

Up close and far away

The number one mistake I see companies make in designing a logo is not considering its range of uses. I can just see the marketing team picking the winning logo winner in an aseptic conference room, under artificial light, looking at a sample that's about 6 inches square. What they fail to realize though is that that same logo must appear in outdoor signage measuring 5 square feet <u>and</u> on its website measuring only 1-inch square.

Consider all the ways your logo will be used—big and small. I once enlarged a client's logo from 4 square inches to 5 square feet and mounted it to the outside of a building. I then drove by the building at 60 miles per hour to test how visible the logo would be. The reason? The client was going to begin advertising on billboards, and I wanted to make sure the logo registered well with the drive-by audience.

Fax it to yourself

If you'll use your new logo on a fax cover sheet, try faxing the logo to yourself as a test. I've received faxes from businesses that looked like they had a huge inkblot in the corner. I later found out that this inkblot was their award-winning logo that doesn't fax worth a darn.

Publish design standards

I'm not talking corporate manuals here. But I do believe in recording the standards for your brand. This branding standards document should cover:

- Sizes
- Colors
- Fonts & typestyles
- Locations or placements

It could just be a 3-ring binder with examples of how you want your logo/etc. to appear. This is a great resource for all internal staff and also could help when it comes time for training.

Don't forget about the sounds of your brand

When you consider brand elements, don't forget the sounds of your brand. Background music. On-hold messaging. These branding elements appeal to our ears, yet sometimes they don't. There's a cool coffee bar near

---

Branding Elements checklist

Here's a checklist of some of the more common **branding** elements your company might use. Check off those that you have already and circle those that are needed.

- ○ Company name
- ○ Taglines
- ○ Division & subsidiary names
- ○ Product & service names
- ○ Trademarks
- ○ Fonts & typestyles
- ○ Logos
- ○ Color schemes
- ○ Music & sounds
- ○ Smells & fragrances

my office. Funky décor, great atmosphere, it's almost perfect, except for the music. I'd best describe it as grunge with an extreme edge. You can tell the "20-something" wait staff likes it, but they aren't customers—they *have* to come back tomorrow. What about the rest of us who can take our business to three other coffee bars in a 6-block radius?

Another company I call on the phone plays rap over its on-hold system. I don't know about you, but I believe there's more to music than 3 bad chords

Branding Vehicles checklist

Here is a checklist of some of the more common **vehicles** a company uses in its branding efforts. Again, check off those you already have and circle those that are needed.

- O Business cards & letterhead
- O Envelopes
- O Premiums
- O Annual reports
- O Promotional brochures & flyers
- O Advertisements
- O Packaging
- O All company signage including directional signs
- O Storefronts & store interiors
- O Reception area signage
- O Conference & board rooms
- O Websites
- O Business vehicles (sales, service, delivery)
- O Uniforms
- O Trade show booths & banners
- O Your building's exterior appearance
- O On-hold messaging
- O Store background music

and rotten lyrics. I hate being on hold with that company! And their relationship with me suffers ever so slightly each time I call.

For more comprehensive branding checklists, visit:
www.emergemarketing.com/publications

Remember...

In the end, hold your branding efforts to the highest standard possible. Keep it of the highest quality you can afford and consistent across all mediums. Your customers (both current and new) will thank you for it.

Tools To Go

○ Think long and hard about what brand image you want your company to portray.

○ Your name is one of the most important branding elements at your disposal. Choose it wisely.

○ Take steps to legally protect your most valuable branding elements.

○ Always have a logo, even if it's a simple one. Some people need pictures to help them remember.

○ Craft a lucid tagline then marry it up with your company name and logo wherever possible.

○ Consider the wide array of branding elements at your disposal then work to keep them upgraded and consistent.

"If you wish to persuade me, you must think my thoughts, feel my feelings and speak my words."

Cicero,
Roman Orator

Chapter 15

12 Tips to Help You Write Better Copy

If you're looking for one marketing tool that can educate, persuade and sell your customers, look no further than the words you use in your marketing. No other tool is so powerful, so persuasive. That's because with any marketing vehicle you use, whether it's ads, direct mail, websites, emails, billboards, T.V. commercials, radio, or just a 2-line directory listing, it's your words that capture the audience's attention.

But before you put any words to paper, consider this: every reader arrives at your copy carrying with them a lifetime of experiences. It's from this perspective that you have one chance to rein them in. If your words are hollow or miss their mark, you've blown your chance.

Here then are 12 ways to give your sales copy a booster shot. Follow these tried and true tactics, and your copy will instantly connect with your readers:

1. Be honest

- *Plop, plop, fizz, fizz, oh what a relief it is©.* (Alka Seltzer)
- *That's what Campbell's Soup is, mmm, mmm good©.* (Campbell's Soup)
- *Betcha can't eat just one©.* (Lay's Potato Chips)
- *Rice a Roni, the San Francisco treat©.* (Rice a Roni)
- *Gets the red out©.* (Visine)
- *Winston tastes good, like a cigarette should©.* (Winston Cigarettes)

Being a baby boomer, I have a raft of these marketing messages tattooed on my brain. I also count among my closest friends Mr. Whipple, Madge and the elderly lady in the Wendy's commercials who barked "Where's the beef?". These confidantes earned my trust by being totally honest with me as they entered my childhood in 30-second vignettes.

Contrast these people with the hundreds of schmaltzy telemarketers who've interrupted my dinner asking "How ya doing?" even though they don't care to hear my answer. Or the mailed timeshare offers that grandly offer me a free unit, even though I must endure a tedious presentation and hounding from the sales person upon my return. The point of all this is to show how folks in my generation have become calloused from a lifetime of marketing. Yet, consider our children.

Kids today play host to a constant barrage of television, radio and direct mail marketing efforts—from birth. Marketing has increased exponentially so that they now, in addition to all the traditional marketing vehicles, are bombarded by a slew of new vehicles including:

○ Websites
○ Spam emails
○ ATM teller machines
○ Special event marketing
○ Movie theatre trailers
○ Broadcast faxes
○ Video trailers
○ Sponsored events and venues

And many others too numerous to mention.

And as if that wasn't enough, I've just learned that one enterprising company is developing splatter pads for urinals that are imprinted with a company's logo and advertising message. Yikes! I don't know about you, but I feel jaded by marketers—and I'm one of 'em!

The sad fact is that people today are besieged with so many competing marketing messages that they've developed a protective layer of disbelief. That's why you've got to be honest in your copy. Besides being a good way to live your life, honesty acts as an anchor for your marketing campaign. Let's face it, if people find your marketing messages unbelievable, or your products don't deliver on the promises you make, what chance of success do you have?

2. Study your audience

When it comes to knowing your customers, you can never have enough information. In fact, marketing should really be looked at as the ongoing effort to start and continue dialogues with a variety of people.

Good marketers study their buyers much like a psychiatrist studies her patient. As the psychiatrist struggles to understand this person's inner workings she asks "Who is this person? How did he get here? What's he feeling?", so must the marketer ask these questions of his target audience. If the marketer truly comprehends the answers to these questions, he understands the depth of his subject, and can design marketing programs that capture this audience's attention. Open dialogues in your marketing, because they are the most effective way to get to know your audience's motivations.

3. Know your audience's level

This is especially important if your marketing is business-to-business. Before you write a word of copy, you'll want to know how high up in an organization—what level—these people are.

I once wrote some copy for a client that organized conferences for the information technology (IT) industry. After the president had reviewed my copy he turned to me and said "Jay, you didn't aim high enough." What he meant was that I had used language and nuance that appealed to a mid-level manager—not a Chief Executive Officer, our target. I had used words like "fast", "efficient" and "results-oriented". Yet these don't register with a Chief Executive Officer the same as "return on investment" and "company value".

As you sit down to write copy for your marketing effort, consider these questions:

○ What level is the company I'm targeting? (Is it a Fortune 500 company? Middle-market? Small Business? Bootstrapping, entrepreneurial 1-person shop?)

○ What level is the person I'm targeting? (Is he an Executive? Director? Manager? Assistant? Owner? Silent partner?)

○ What title does this person have?

○ Whom does he/she report to?

○ What daily concerns does a person at this level have?

4. Speak to your audience's pain

To be truly successful at copy writing, the talented marketer must tap into a buyer's raw emotions—his *pain*. Try comparing these two sets of copy:

---

1. "The Plex 2000 helps you sleep better."

2. "We know you worry about sleeping. Maybe you start worrying right after dinner, or it could be as you're putting the kids to bed. It starts slowly, like a train heading out of a station. But it's there—a nagging doubt that fills your stomach with a numbing pit. And you just can't seem to shake it from your mind. Pretty soon the fear washes over you, and your heart begins to race.

 If only you had a better bed, you know you'd lazily drift off to sleep, but you don't. Now, maybe it's time to think seriously about the Plexi 2000."

Which copy section draws you in better? When you write marketing copy, you have to crawl figuratively into your reader's brain and grasp the *pain* he feels every day.

Is he scared? Worried? Stressed? Starved for time? Is he missing out on family time? Does he wish he were in love? Does he just want some attention? Does he want to be recognized for his hard work? Is he facing money pressures? Is he embarrassed? Are coworkers ridiculing him? Do his loved ones worry about him? What's happening to his health? Is he losing sleep? Does he feel sad? Feeling—really *feeling*—your audience's pain helps you select words that bypass the prospect's brain and head straight for his heart. Once you empathize with the pain he's feeling, you've made a friend for life.

Allow me to test you again. I'd like you to read the sentences below and take note of those that truly capture the pain someone might feel:
- *Do you need marketing services?*
- *Are you looking for better marketing?*
- *Are your competitors embarrassing you in the market?*

- *When was the last time you were really proud of the way your marketing materials looked?*
- *Do you live in constant fear that your competitor will steal your biggest customer?*
- *Are you frustrated because you're in charge of marketing, but that's not where your expertise is?*

The last four do the best job of uncovering the raw emotions, don't they? Now, think about your business and see if you can answer these questions:

1. What pain does your audience feel?

_____

_____

_____

_____

2. How does this pain complicate their lives?

_____

_____

_____

_____

3. In what ways does your business (or your product) eliminate this pain?

_____

_____

_____

_____

5. Know your key messages

Sometimes marketers, staring at a blank sheet of paper, feel overwhelmed by the task of writing copy. How can they write a paragraph, let alone a whole brochure?

But I believe they're feeling that way because they've skipped an important step in the copy writing process. They've gone straight from the "We need to start marketing" phase to the "I need to write 3 paragraphs of copy by noon tomorrow" phase without thinking strategically about what they'll say.

An intermediate step before ever writing a word of copy, is to determine your *key messages*. Remember back in English class how we were trained to first write out a paper's thesis before actually writing the paper? This thesis statement was the overall argument you wanted to assert—the central point of the paper. That's really what key messages are in your marketing copy, your thesis statements. They're the central points you'll communicate in this written piece.

So, before writing any copy at all, jot down the three key messages you want to communicate. If you can identify these key messages first, I think you'll find that writing copy is a much easier proposition.

Figure 6 is a handy form you can use to help collect these key messages for your company.

After you've completed this form, keep it nearby for when you develop new marketing communications. All future marketing copy, whether it's for ads, brochures, direct mail, client letters, scripts, on-hold messaging—you name it—should be written with this completed form sitting beside you.

Figure 6:

Key Messages Matrix
Company Audiences (Which types of companies do we want to attract?)	• • •
People Audiences (Which people or titles do we want to appeal to?)	• • •
Pain (What difficulties do our prospects face? What emotional pain do they suffer without our product?)	• • •
Features (What makes our product or service superior to the competition?)	• • •
Benefits (How do we make people's lives easier?)	• • •
Competitive Advantages (What makes our company superior to the competition?)	• • •
Key Messages (What are the 3 most important arguments you want to make in this piece?)	• • •
Words You Want to Own (What words do you want people to associate with your company?)	• • •

6. Focus on benefits

24 hour hot lines. Overnight delivery. 10 gigabytes of memory. What do these things mean to the red hot prospect—NOTHING! That's because they're all *features*. Features give the prospect details about the product, but they don't indicate what the prospect gains from it. Those are *benefits*, and they're at the heart of a prospect's needs. For example:

> "Save $1,000 over the course of a year."
>
> "Contact us when it fits into your schedule."
>
> "Store even the largest files and never worry about available storage."

These are all examples of benefits that powerfully involve the reader in your copy. Each of these has an emotional payoff (save money, convenience, and eliminate worry) to the reader—in short, they make your audience *feel* better.

If you're unsure how to link features or benefits, try this exercise. First, write down a descriptive phrase for a business (i.e. legal services). Then ask yourself "When a prospect buys this, what does she really get?" (i.e. fewer headaches, less wasted time, more money from settlements). Then link the two with the phrase "so you get—".

So, using this example, you'd write the phrase:

> "We provide legal services **so you get** more money from your settlements."

I once asked a management consultant what his client ended up with, and his answer surprised me. "Jay," he said, "because I help this company's president meet his tax deadlines, he *gets his boat in the water in time for the fishing opener*." If you're a fisherman out there, you know how important this is!

To spark your thinking on the benefits you offer others, I've developed two charts that list some of the more common benefits. See if there aren't some here you can borrow:

Some common benefits to a _company_		
Sales • Increase sales • Increase market share • Create more loyal customers	**Speed** • Faster decisions • Faster product delivery • Faster inventory turns	**Problem avoidance** • Experience/knowledge • Avoid litigation • Identify risks
Management support • Objectivity • Adjunct staff	**Higher productivity** • Better work flows • More motivated employees • Fewer errors	**Personal satisfaction** • Prestige of working w/your company • Safe place to talk • Mental stimulation

Some common benefits to a _consumer_	
Wants to gain... • Advancement • Popularity • Credibility • Vacations/family time	**Wants to save...** • Time • Money • Embarrassment
Wants to... • Win others' affection • Improve themselves • Resist domination by others	**Wants to be...** • A recognized authority • Up-to-date • A good parent

7. Use power marketing words

Some words get a more visceral reaction from people. Unfortunately, many are four-letter words, but leading marketing experts have discovered that certain words really pack a wallop. Here are 35 of the most powerful words known to marketing. Sprinkle them throughout your marketing materials, and you'll <u>benefit</u> from better <u>results</u> and <u>faster</u> sales (that's three right there!)

35 of the Most Powerful Marketing Words

You/your	Benefit	Now
Results	How to	Proof
Health	Love	Only
Easy	Fun	Just for you
Proven	Finally	Exclusive
Free	Discount	Limited
New	Special	First time
Now	Breakthrough	Bonus
Save	100%	Faster
Money	Secret	Immediately
Safe	Last chance	Quick
Guarantee	Unique	

If you need more, check out the book *Words that Sell* by Richard Bayan (Contemporary Books, 1984). This handy reference guide lists over 2,500 high-powered words and breaks them down by connotation—a very valuable tool.

8. Write 'head-turning' headlines

Whether you're writing an ad, a direct mail piece, a press release or a sales letter, the most widely read part of it will be the headline. I call this your "head turner'" and if you've ever watched someone intently read something, you probably know what I mean. She'll quizzically cock her head to the side as she comes across something that piques her interest.

When you see your reader do this, it means they're thinking, "Wow, I never thought of it that way." Strive to get this reaction in every headline you write. Why? Because it means you have your audience's full and undivided attention, and their permission to continue.

> *"...five times as many people read the headlines as read the body copy."*
>
> David Ogilvy, Legendary advertising writer

I once wrote a press release for a manufacturing company that specialized in thermoformed plastics. During my information gathering meetings, the president pointed out that his company had a reputation for taking on the unconventional jobs his competitors refused to bid on. One such job was to manufacture a small number of oversized bugs, and another was to produce some innovative masks that were used in a local theatre production. As he related these war stories, I sensed this was a resourceful manufacturer who didn't shy away from an unusual project. So, I wrote and distributed a press release with the headline:

"We like Weird!"

The result? The release was a smashing success and was picked up by every major daily, weekly and monthly business publication in the Twin Cities. In addition, several national trade publications ran articles on the company. Why did this happen? I believe one big reason was because of the head-turning headline. Editors were so drawn in by the release's compelling headline that they felt compelled to read more about this company.

9. Break it up with subheads & bullets

Today's busy reader skims when he reads; there just isn't time to read every word. I personally read 3 newspapers each day, but to say I read each of them is inaccurate. I skim them. So, to help your readers find exactly what they're looking for, use subheads.

A subhead is a type of headline that introduces a section of copy. The subhead for this section of copy is called "Break it up with subheads & bullets". When a reader skims your copy, you make it easier for him by providing subheads. That way, the reader can review large amounts of text and choose the copy he's most interested in reading.

If you've ever received a memo or flyer that consisted of just a solid block of copy, what was your initial reaction? If you're like me, you said to yourself "Oh man, I'm not going to read *all that*." Subheads make your reader feel that your copy is surmountable. And that's a key first step in getting him to read it.

10. Give 'em a call-to-action

It's not enough to just rattle off your product's features and benefits. You must go one step further by telling your reader *exactly what you want her to do next*. Too often I see marketing materials that effectively present a company, yet leave the next step up to their audience to figure out. And when I ask why the materials don't include a call-to-action, I'm met with the response "Oh, we don't want to be too pushy."

Pshaw! Remember that your buyer is probably reading your copy while watching a football game and keeping an eye on Junior. If you're lucky, you only have half this person's attention and you might not have it for long.

Folks, we marketers are in the business of convincing people to take action, so it is our obligation to tell them what action we want them to take.

That's where a *call-to-action* comes in. A call-to-action is a highly motivating statement that tells the reader exactly what action she should take next. Here are some examples of highly motivating calls-to-action:

• *So, call (888) 555-1212 today and learn how these shirt-pocket organizers can simplify your life.*

• *Visit www.emergemarketing.com and click on "About Us" to learn more.*

• *"Send us a check for $9, using the self-enclosed envelope, and start enjoying these Special Reports today."*

If you're not sure what your call-to-action might be, I advise our clients to map out the typical information-gathering steps a prospect goes through. It might look like this:

Step 1
Call for a brochure

Step 2
Study/Evaluate Literature

Step 3
Request a quote or meeting

Step 4
Purchase

By doing this, you identify all the possible call-to-actions you can use. So, using the map above as an example, you could craft a call-to-action around Step #3 that reads:

"Call us today and request a quote from our estimator."

11. Offer several ways to respond

All too often a business assumes its prospects are all at the same buying stage. But that's not true is it? Two different respondents to a direct mail campaign may have entirely different motivations. One could just be curious about your product, while the other has a pressing need with a deadline.

As you write call to actions, face the fact that your buyers are in a multitude of different buying stages. Some are raring to put down the cash and buy that sucker. Others are almost ready to buy, but need to do a bit more due diligence. Some are uncomfortable about shelling out all that money and need an assurance that they have a recourse if they're dissatisfied. And others are downright skeptical. They won't buy no matter what anybody says.

How do you write one call-to-action that appeals to all these people?

You don't. You write several. By offering a variety of different ways to respond, you can better appeal to a larger audience as well as gauge your respondents' interest level.

For example, at the bottom of a flyer you might use a checkbox like this:

Check the box if:

○ You'd like a rep to contact you.

○ You'd like to receive a brochure.

○ You'd like someone to contact you about getting a quote.

○ You want to know more about our unconditional, money back guarantee.

Or, in an email newsletter, you might use these three options:

1. Visit us at www.emergemarketing.com for more information

2. Email us at lipe@emergemarketing.com with specific questions or

3. Click here to email this to a friend.

Understand that all buyers are not equal, and craft your response options accordingly.

12. Give them an opt-out

These days you'll do your marketing a great service by offering an *opt-out* option. All an opt-out does is give the recipient, every time they receive a marketing communication, the opportunity to discontinue receiving it. It could look like this:

You are currently subscribed to Emerge Marketing's e-Marketing Newsletter as: lipe@emergemarketing.com To unsubscribe click here

Or, it could look like this:

OPT OUT?
If you've received this newletter by mistake or want to be taken off the list, please email me at lipe@emergemarketing.com or call (612) 824-4833 and leave a message.

With more and more buyers demanding control over the buying process these days, offering an opt-out clause in all your marketing materials puts the power in your buyers' hands.

Remember...

Don't believe the pundits who have sounded the death knell for words in our culture. Persuasive and motivating copy is very much alive in the marketing field—indeed it's still a prime motivator for people to buy. Know your audience well, then write copy that appeals directly to their self-interests. If you tap into a prospect's pain, using the right words, you'll generate a response, and that's an important step for us marketers.

Tools To Go

- ○ Study your audience—and know the level they're at within a company.
- ○ Speak to their pain.
- ○ Develop your key messages and then record them in a Key Messages matrix.
- ○ Focus on benefits—how you'll make your readers' lives easier.
- ○ Use power-marketing words.
- ○ Focus on your headlines—they're, by far, the most important copy you'll write.
- ○ Always provide a call-to-action, offer several ways to respond, and provide an opt-out.

"Try not.
Do, or do not.
There is no try."

Yoda, from *The Empire
Strikes Back*

Chapter 16

Secrets to Search Engine Positioning

Much has been written about websites for the growing company. But, I find a real dearth of information about search engines, which to my mind are just as important. Here then is some basic information about search engines and what they can do for your site. But, beware. This field is changing so rapidly that it would behoove you to subscribe to several e-magazines (ezines) just to stay on top of this field (I've listed several in the Resources Directory at the end of the book).

Search engines...huh?

Imagine for a moment your company owns a kiosk in the mall. And on that kiosk, you've posted award-winning pictures and marketing copy about your product. This is a great marketing tool, right? Maybe.

But now imagine that your kiosk sits, not in the middle of the mall, but off in a dark and dusty corner where noone ever goes. By my reckoning this marketing tool is a downright waste of money.

Much the same principle applies with websites. A high-quality website (the kiosk in this example) by itself, doesn't guarantee success. How many prospects visit that site and the qualified level of these prospects do.

Below are some tips and techniques to ensure search engines—a key ingredient to web success—drive targeted traffic to your site.

Why you need search engines

A recent survey in *Target Marketing* magazine ranked the top ways people found websites:

Search Engines	46%	By accident	2%
Random surfing	20%	TV spots	1%
Word-of-mouth	20%	Targeted Email	1%
Magazine ads	4%	Other	6%

And according to a GVU users survey, 84.8% of global surfers use search engines to find goods and services. Clearly, search engines are a top method for finding websites.

Furthermore, many people familiar with your site (e.g. customers) already have your address memorized or bookmarked. That means people who use search engines to find your site are more likely to be new prospects.

Finally, search engines are a relevant and credible way for people to find you. Some methods (banner ads come to mind) have lost credibility over the years. But search engines are still regarded as a fast and objective way to find what you're looking for on the web.

All this means that search engines are a golden opportunity to attract new traffic to your site—one of the key reasons you chose to build a website, right?

Here Mr. Spider...

To keep current on the millions of websites out there, search engines employ *spiders*. These spiders are super-fast page scanners that automatically visit web pages, catalog the information and then store these web pages in a database. So, when a user visits a search engine and types in a keyword, the engine scans its database for relevant web pages. Based on indexing the spider has done after visiting your site, your site may then be suggested as a site for the user to click on.

As a marketer, your goal then is to organize and present your website in such a way that, when the spiders do visit, they capture and catalogue your web pages to yield the highest possible rankings for your site. If you're wondering what the most common spiders are, visit this site to learn more:

   http://searchenginewatch.com/webmasters/spiderchart.html

Now read on for some tips and techniques to help you attract spiders. But beware, you have to think like a spider to attract one!

Strategize on search engines before designing your site

Good graphic design goes a long way towards welcoming new users to your site. But, it can also sabotage search engine optimization. If you don't strike a balance between website design and search engine optimization, you'll end up like the great looking kiosk stuck in the corner of the mall.

As a first step, before website design has begun, develop a brief plan for search engine optimization.

For starters, answer these questions:

○ Are we committed to search engines as a viable way to generate site traffic?

○ Which search engines do we want to appear in regularly?

○ What ranking level will we be satisfied with? (I wouldn't settle for anything less than Top 20)

Design a Spider-Friendly Site

To develop a spider-friendly site, follow these basic rules when developing your site:

1. Reduce your graphics

Spiders are graphic-illiterate. When a spider scans a graphic, all it sees is a blank spot. If it isn't text, it isn't seen. So, if you're loading your front page with a lot of graphics or fancy flash animation, all the spider sees is a blank page.

One of the hardest things I've had to do as a web marketer is get over my love of graphics. You see, graphics may grab a human's attention in the printed world, but they'll go wholly unnoticed by a spider. The copy on your pages is what the spider sees, so I recommend using well-crafted copy (featuring choice keywords) throughout your site with a minimum of graphics. Save these graphics for when you really need 'em.

2. Be liberal with your contact info

Since a spider sees the copy on each page, why not build your company contact information into the footer of every page? This helps 3 ways:

1) Search engines will grab this information and index it as well.

2) People often print off pages from a site. Having your contact info there at the bottom helps them get in touch with you when all they have is a hard copy.

3) Putting a physical address on each page increases credibility.

3. Use text over graphics

Below, Ecolab uses plenty of text and even subdivides the text by markets, business divisions and headlines. Using this approach increases the odds a spider will index your site high in its database.

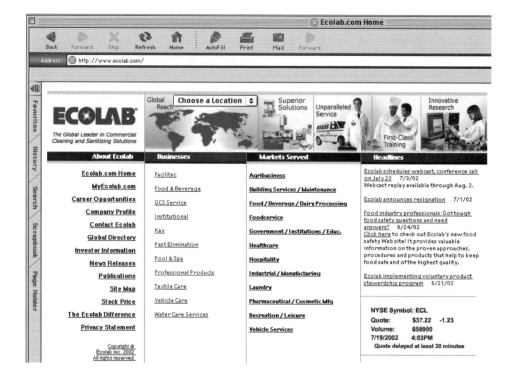

4. Choose a Strong Title

Your title bar appears at the top of your browser menu and is "E&Y International Home" in this example:

Whenever a user clicks onto your website, or into a section of your site, they'll get a title bar for that location. To program your title bar, you (or your site developer) will write some simple code like this:

```
<TITLE>E&amp;YInternationalHome</TITLE>
```

What you put in your title bar is VERY important for several reasons

1) It appears as the bookmark title for those who bookmark your site. Like this:

2) It appears as the link title (blue highlighted & underlined) when your search results come back after performing a search <u>and</u>

3) Search engine spiders give high priority to your title and expect your title to be descriptive of your site's content.

So for example, if your site has as its title "Flyaway Travel", then that's what will appear in my bookmarks. That's fine, but wouldn't it be better if the title also described what you do? Like maybe "Flyaway Travel—Cheap Domestic Airfares". That way, when I come across your bookmark after some time, I am reminded of who you are and what you offer.

Remember too that if you don't put a title in the title bar, your site title bar reads as "Page 1" or "home page".

If your business is regional, you may want to underscore this trading area in your title bar. For example, if your consulting company is regionally-based, you could design your title bar to read:

Superdupe Financial Advisors — Minneapolis, MN

This calls out the regional expertise of your business and helps distinguish it from more national (and pricier) firms. One final note: try to keep your title to around 8 words or less.

Keep in mind that it's how your *customers* and *prospects* see your business that counts. Even though you really like your tagline, if it doesn't help your site register high in the search engines, it's not good marketing.

5. Improve your meta tags

Meta tags are hidden descriptions of your web pages that appear only in the embedded source code. They're used to point search engine spiders to the right places. Meta tags are very powerful because they actually help control how your web pages are displayed in the search engines. You can use up to 1,000 characters in a meta tag and this includes letters, spaces and commas.

Here's an example of how a meta tag might be programmed:

<meta name="Description" CONTENT="Custom photo albums and branding products, for business, resorts, schools, national parks, cruises, and more.">

<meta name="KeyWords" CONTENT="extended exposure, exposures, scrap books, journals, bon-voyage, bon voyage, commemorative, promotional, personalized photo albums, family reunions, corporate branding, disposable cameras, branding products, promotional products, promotions, advertising specialties, agfa, disposable cameras, real estate gifts, national park products, travel souvenirs, resort souvenirs, souveniers, custom photo albums, travel advertising, creative solutions, creative advertising, vacation stuff, incentive products, thank you gifts, business promotions, asta marketing services, travel bags, st paul, st. paul, Minneapolis, mn">
<meta name="revisit-after" content="5 days">
<meta name="robot" CONTENT="ALL">
<meta name="rating" CONTENT="General">
<meta name="distribution" content="Global">
<meta name="robots" content="INDEX">
<meta name="Template Author" content="Ed Kohler - http://www.4factors.com/">
<meta name="Creation Date" content="Saturday, May 5, 2001">
<meta name="Last Update" content=" Saturday, May 5, 2001">

If you need some help in developing a meta tag for your site, the following site has developed a 'Meta Tag Generator':

http://www.haystackinaneedle.com/recommend/genmeta.html

Notice that keywords are a chief component of your meta tags. When you feature the right keywords in your meta tag, you'll end up driving traffic to your site.

I should note here that a recent trend towards meta tag keyword spamming, especially by pornography sites, has driven some search engines to place less emphasis on meta tags, and more on page content. Stay tuned.

6. Keyword hints

Most websites let you list up to 875 characters in your keyword section. Here are some hints on finding the right keywords for your site:

Hint: Visit www.wordtracker.com This site has compiled a database of terms that people search for. You can enter keywords into their database, and they'll tell you how often people search for them. They'll also tell you how many competing sites use those keywords. So, if you're contemplating using 'dry cleaning' as a keyword for your site, you can check on its popularity.

Using this handy site, you can then build a keyword and submissions strategy around selected keywords.

Hint: Use the long and short versions of keywords (e.g. consult, consulting, and consultants).

Hint: Use key phrases to describe your business. So instead of using 'Internet', I also use 'Internet consultants'.

Hint: Don't forget to include common misspellings as keywords. For example, if your company is in the marketing business, consider including 'marekting' or 'markeitng'. That way, when someone inadvertently misspells or mis-types a search term for a search engine, it will still list your site in the search results.

Hint: A way to track your site's ranking ability in various search engines is to include a fictitious term in your keywords. So for example, if you're a manufacturer of steel products, include a term like 'oxshards'. After submitting your site and getting a visit from the spider, visit the search engine and do a search using 'oxshards'. Your site should come up in the search results.

7. Check into your competitor's keywords

You no doubt already know what some of your keywords should be. They might be products, services, business categories and maybe even geography terms (if you're an accountant in Chicago, try 'Chicago Accountants' as a key phrase).

Another way to find out popular keywords is to visit your competitors' sites. While at your competitor's site, click on View ➡ Source in your browser's navigation bar.

The code you're now looking at will contain the keywords for this site. Search through these keywords to determine which you're already using and which might be good to add to your keywords. Why reinvent the wheel? Take advantage of someone else's existing expertise.

8. Weave keywords into page content

Once you've determined the most important keywords for your site, you need to weave them into your site's body copy. The more frequently these keywords appear, and the nearer they appear to the beginning of a page, the greater the likelihood of high search engine placement.

Your site's home page should contain the greatest concentration of keywords. On this page, weave those words and phrases you think searchers will use most to find your site. If you're a plumbing supply company use the word "plumbing" (obviously) but also "plumbing supplies".

With recent changes in how search engines find and rank sites, keyword density is sure to become even more of a science.

The Top Search Engines

This is an ever-shifting field of competitors, but today the most influential search engines are:

Top Search Engines (as of Summer '02)

Site Name	Address
Google	www.google.com
Altavista	www.altavista.com
Inktomi	www.inktomi.com
AOL Search	www.search.aol.com
Hotbot	www.hotbot.lycos.com
MSN Search	www.search.msn.com
Netscape Search	www.search.netscape.com
AKA Direct Hit	www.teoma.com
Lycos	www.searchservices.lycos.com

How do you submit to a search engine?

Every search engine treats site submissions differently. In some, submission links appear right on the search engine's front page. For example, Alta Vista (www.altavista.com) has a link on its front page that looks like this:

About AltaVista | Terms Of Use | **Privacy Policy** | Help | Contact Us
Submit A Site | Advertise With Us | Jobs | List Your Products | A CMGI Company

Other search engines make you dig a bit deeper to find the site submission procedures. After you've found the place to submit your site, most search engines will ask you for this information:

> - Your site's web address (also called a URL with the format http:/www._____.com)
>
> - Your personal email (so they can get back to you once it's been indexed)

That's all they need to know. Then they will add your site address to their querying code and you'll get a visit from its spider.

How long does it take for your web page submissions to be indexed? That all depends on the workload for the search engine's spiders. But generally, the following timeframes apply for getting approval for your submission to certain search engines:

Search Engine	Approval Timing
Altavista	1 - 2 weeks
HotBot	2 weeks
Excite, Lycos	4 weeks
Google	4 - 6 weeks
Infoseek, Go	6 - 8 weeks
Webcrawler	12 weeks

If after these times pass and you don't seem to be getting any results from your submission, I'd recommend resubmitting.

Some differences between search engines and directories

Now that you know a bit more about search engines, let's talk about *directories*. Here are some ways they differ from search engines:

	Search Engine	Directory
Cost	Free	Costs in the vicinity of 0-$300 yr.
How it's edited/indexed	Robot Edited	Human edited
Resubmission	Best to resubmit every year	No need to resubmit
Content	• Unabridged content • Whole site indexed and searchable	• Abridged—usually only lists home page

How to submit to directories

Unlike search engines, directories won't find your site if you don't tell them about it. They don't use spiders to scour the Internet for new pages. So with directories, you have to actively seek them out and submit.

Also, they usually only search the front page. Additional pages can be submitted for a price. Some of the top directories today are:

Top Directories (as of Summer '02)	
Site Name	**Address**
Looksmart	www.looksmart.com
Yahoo	www.yahoo.com
Ask Jeeves	www.askjeeves.com

In addition there are regional directories you might want to check out. In the Twin Cities, a well-known regional directory is www.twincities.com. Also, don't overlook your industry directories and member directories.

For example, if you're in the travel industry www.astanet.com (the American Society of Travel Agents' site) might be worth checking into.

One other submission method: Pay-per-Click

There is one other type of search engine that can build your traffic. It's called a *pay-per-click* or *paid submission* search engine. At these search engines, you open an account, make a deposit of between $10-$100 ($50 is the deposit for Overture.com (formerly GoTo.com) and then list your keywords.

What makes these sites unique is that you 'bid' on the keywords you'd like to have steer viewers to your site. Each keyword has a market value based upon the relative demand for it among other people using the site. Bids for keywords can be made for as low as 5 cents on Overture.com, and as low as 1 cent on most other pay-per-click sites.

After you successfully bid on certain keywords, then you submit your site and pay for each click on your chosen keywords.

So for example, if you're a manufacturer of plastic thermoforming, you might bid on the term 'plastic thermoforming' for 5 cents per click-through. Each time a visitor types in 'plastic thermoforming' and your site pops up, your account is charged 5 cents.

Maybe you're a business consultant and you want to bid on 'business consultant'. You'd probably find that it's valued higher, say at $1.00 per click-through. The value of any keyword on these sites is based on its relative popularity. The more popular a keyword is, the more you can expect to pay for it.

One benefit to these sites is that you only pay for results. You only get charged for those searches that use the terms you've bid on.

You also have flexibility to change your keywords frequently. After a time, you can log onto a member's area and review the traffic each keyword delivers to your site. If any of your keywords aren't carrying their weight, just change them to what you think will.

Top Pay-per-Click sites:	
Site Name	**Address**
Overture (formerly Go To)	www.overture.com
Ah-Ha	www.ah-ha.com
Power Search Express	www.PowerSearchExpress.com
Search Hound	www.SearchHound.com
Search Feed	www.SearchFeed.com

One final note: as of Spring 2002, more and more free search engines are moving towards a pay-per-click format. Google has just added a new pay-per-click feature and others are expected to follow.

Stay on top of this fast-moving industry by frequenting these sites:

www.searchenginewatch.com

www.searchengineguide.com

www.searchengineheadlines.com

Track your traffic

One thing I've learned is that rigorous analysis is a key to marketing success. That means you'll want to build metrics into your search engine ranking effort. Simply put, these metrics help you track what you're getting from this effort. In web terms you'll want to know:

• **How many**—How many unique visitors are we getting? How many page views are we getting? How many people are returning?

• **Who**—Who are these people? What search engines are they coming from? What are their typical web-hosting arrangements? What keywords are they using?

• **Where**—Where do they go in your site? Are they coming for the free stuff? Are they reading lots of pages or just a few? Which links are they clicking on?

All in all, we've found the most valuable metrics to be:

Top 10 Web Metrics

1. Unique visitors per day
2. Average page views per visitor
3. Most popular pages on the site
4. Common search phrases used
5. Most requested pages
6. Most common site entry point
7. Most common site exit point
8. Top referring sites
9. Busiest days and times of day for your site
10. Page views per day

The best way to answer these questions is to use Web Analytics software. These sites help you accurately and powerfully analyze your Web site traffic. We use Superstats (www.superstats.com) and have been very pleased with it. Here's a sample report you can generate from this site:

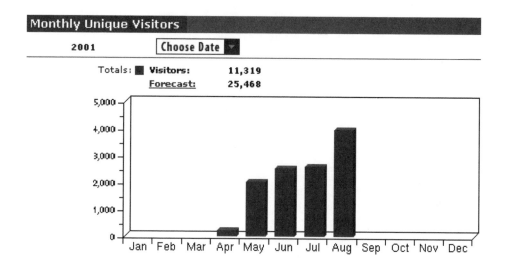

Using a program like this helps answer these questions on a monthly, weekly or even daily basis. There is a cost for this service, but it's well worth it to get up-to-the-minute feedback on your site.

Use professionals

If it seems like this is complicated, it is. This is a whole new marketing vehicle to many of us and that's why you'll want to consider using outside professionals in your web marketing efforts. They can help you develop marketing strategies and then implement those strategies. So you can just concentrate on running your business.

Remember...

50-85% of all website visits result from the use of a search engine. It's estimated that 150 million visitors frequent one search engine alone, Google. To tap into this huge (and growing) traffic stream, you've got to be in this game.

Tools To Go

○ Search engines can fuel your site traffic.

○ Strategize on search engines <u>before</u> designing your site.

○ Make your site design spider-friendly.

○ Use text over graphics.

○ Choose a strong title tag.

○ Use keyword-heavy meta tags.

○ Weave keywords and phrases into page content.

○ Submit your finished site to the best search engines. If you don't get visited within the guidelines, contact them again.

○ Pay-per-click sites are gaining popularity. The days of exclusively free traffic appear to be waning.

○ Track your traffic with an analytics package.

○ Use professionals in this area. It's too important to tackle yourself.

"In prosperity be
prudent, in adversity
be patient."

Anonymous

Chapter 17

How To Market Your Company During a Recession

If you study the U.S. economy from 1950-2000, you'll see that we, as a nation, have suffered through nine recessions. And those nine recessions account for 94 months in total, or 14 percent of those 50 years. In addition, the average recession has lasted 11 months with two recessions, those beginning in 1975 and 1982, lasting 16 months.

With these statistics as a backdrop, one thing is certain—all small business owners must know how to market their company during a recession. It's only a matter of time before you'll find yourself in one.

Here are some tips for helping you manage your marketing effort during a slowdown.

Why you should market during a slowdown

The best thing about a slowdown, if there is such a thing, is that the playing field suddenly becomes less crowded. Many companies, needing to conserve cash, will stay on the sidelines during a recession thus creating a golden opportunity for you.

Precisely because other companies are slashing their marketing spending, your best marketing strategy then is to "stay out there" with your marketing. Your messages will cut through the market easier for the simple fact that they won't compete as much for attention. Sure, you may have to scale back your spending, but don't squander this opportunity to stand out from the crowd.

Another reason to continue your marketing efforts throughout a slowdown is to keep the valuable momentum you've built up. Much time, money and effort has been invested to this point and withdrawing from the market blunts this advantage.

When do you start planning?

The time to start planning for the next recession is right now. Since neither you nor I know for certain when the next recession will be, any planning you do now gives you a leg up on your competition when the recession arrives—whether it's tomorrow or years from now. Learn from those of us who've lived through recessions before and found ourselves saying, "If only I'd planned for this."

Smart companies recognize the threat of a recession well before it occurs, and already have a plan in mind to follow. And if you're not the kind who enjoys written plans, at the very least, have in your mind several steps you'll take at the onset of a recession.

Pare down debt

Carrying debt into a recession is like playing Russian Roulette with only one empty chamber; your chances for survival are slim. During a recession, your sales will slow and your receivables cycle will lengthen. To compensate for these things, you'll want to have as much cash on-hand as possible. Any dollar that pays down debt is a dollar that detracts from your cash flow. What you're looking for during a recession is options, and debt subtracts from, not adds to, your options.

Take steps to eliminate your debt before the recession comes and you'll find yourself with more options when the skies darken.

Save now

Money in the bank during a recession is like, well, money in the bank. Any savings you can generate will act as a safety net for you during rough times. I learned this during the 2001-02 recession. Before then, our company had some very good years, and I was tempted to spend all our excess cash on technology and new marketing programs. But, this little voice in the back of my head (probably put there by my parents) kept telling me to save a little each month. So, every time we received payment from a client, I socked away 10%. I wasn't sure what we'd use it for, but I knew we'd need it.

Then, as you know, the rain came in '01. But because of our savings, we were able to continue our marketing programs through the recession without interruption, and even develop a new marketing initiative when some of our competitors were pulling back.

Start saving now and you'll be surprised at how much you'll need those funds during a recession. You may even be able to buy out your competitor. You know—the one who went into the recession with zero savings and a debt load the size of Alaska!

Cash is king

During good times, you don't have to pay as much attention to cash flow. Money flows freely. But during a slowdown you must proactively take steps to free up cash. Here are some strategies to help strengthen your business' cash situation:

1. Insist on down payments

I'm always a little surprised at the number of companies I see that don't collect money up front. With a down payment, you have money in hand, even before your product is manufactured or your service rendered. Can you ask for a first payment to accompany the purchase order, or a "Move Forward Payment" upon signing the contract?

2. Invoice in-process

If you typically bill customers after the job is finished (or after the product is shipped), then you might want to consider billing a portion (typically 50% of the remaining amount) midway through the production. Immediately after the project is finished you can then invoice for the remainder. Remember, the faster you get bills out, the faster you get cash in.

3. Jettison all image marketing programs

Every one of your programs during the recession must work, first and foremost, to generate sales for your company. This isn't the time to launch marketing campaigns that are designed to build image. These softer, more qualitative marketing programs must be back burnered in favor of immediate, sales-building programs.

4. Push out your payment dates

Look hard at your payment cycles to your suppliers. Most vendors our company comes into contact with traditionally use a 30-day payment cycle. Use all of these 30 days to hold onto your cash. I'm not suggesting that you delay payment to these companies. Rather, take every day they give you to pay them—and not a day sooner.

Recycle older campaigns

Chances are you have a file folder full of previous marketing campaigns—old direct mail campaigns, previous email marketing campaigns, telemarketing scripts from days gone by. Now is the time to dust them off and resurrect them. You've invested a lot of intellectual capital in them, why not run them again? This is a cheap and effective way to circumvent creative development charges you'd ordinarily pay thousands of dollars for.

Use broadcast emails

Emails give all companies a low-cost way to promote their companies and products. Add to this the fact that they are easily forwarded by recipients; thus generating an online word-of-mouth phenomenon. Plus, these emails can produce an immediate response to a particular offer. Just as important, emails reduce the time required to launch a promotional campaign. I discovered all this working with a local travel agency.

Towards the end of the week, we'd find ourselves with unsold airline seats to certain destinations. We'd then put out a broadcast email to all subscribers who had asked to be included on these emails (an opt-in list) and within a couple of days, we'd sold the excess inventory. If you need to move merchandise quickly, have limited time offers or discounts, or have built a list of email addresses, develop a simple email campaign. It could prove to be a winner—especially during quiet times.

Keep firing your marketing guns

The tendency in a recession is to reduce the *frequency* of your marketing programs—that's the number of times you employ a particular marketing tool.

For example, if you reduce your direct mailings from eight times to just four times a year, you've cut your frequency in half. That means your prospects will hear from you 50% less often—and you don't want to do that because that's what everyone else is doing.

Instead, why not stay with eight mailings but reduce the costs of each mailing. Print one-sided versus four-page sell sheets. Eliminate enclosures. Print black & white. Reduce paper sizes. Mail third class for postal savings.

Do whatever it takes to reduce the cost of your eight mailings while maintaining the same frequency. This is not easy to do, and takes some creativity, but chopping your frequency is more dangerous. The silence will be deafening to your customers.

Keep 'em purchasing with "bite-sized buys"

During a recession, your selling cycle will be longer. Uncertainty about the future prompts prospects to postpone purchasing, or even considering a decision, until it's absolutely required. To counteract this, give your prospects "bite-sized" ways to purchase your products.

Produce an informational booklet. Develop a sample packet of product. Offer a free trial period. Suggest the client implement just the first phase of a project. All these let people "try a bite" of your company without a long-term commitment. If your product or service delivers on its promises, don't worry—they'll be back for more.

Make more dials

At 15 cents per minute, there are very few marketing vehicles cheaper or more efficient than the phone call. Telephoning during a recession is one very effective way to stay in touch with your audience, while keeping your costs down.

However, let me stress I'm NOT talking about cold-call telemarketing. Although I see that work for some businesses out there, I generally don't recommend it to clients for two reasons:

> • Very little telemarketing is handled professionally.
>
> • Telemarketing has a negative stigma attached to it.

However, your company should use the phone to stay in touch with customers and prospects. These are people who already know you, and view the call as less of an intrusion.

If you call customers and prospects, and use a low-pressure approach, I think the phone can be a very valuable weapon. So, call a couple prospects or customers each week and use any of these approaches:

> • Call to just say "Hi".
> • Follow up mailings with a call.
> • Update your data base information on them.
> • Ask their opinion about something having to do with your business (i.e. your website, marketing materials or a recent mailer they might have received).

Oh, and one last thing—always *take the curse off the call.* When the person answers the phone, and the introductions are out of the way, ask them "Have I caught you at a bad time?" before going further. This gives them the option of taking the call at a later date and creates a favorable impression for your call. Far too many callers don't extend this basic courtesy.

Offer an ironclad guarantee

In a slow economy, people act cautiously and prolong decisions, especially big ones. One way to attack this reluctance is by offering an ironclad guarantee. A money-back guarantee (with no questions asked) is an excellent way to recognize their concerns up front, and prove the confidence you have in your product or service.

I've personally found that when I see a company offer a money back guarantee, I feel much better about doing business with them. Their own confidence rubs off on me and makes me that much more likely to give them a try.

Explore maintenance or used opportunities

As the recession of 1991 lengthened, I noticed more and more clunkers out on the road. You know, cars with rusted out bodies, no hubcaps and taped plastic for windows. And then it hit me—a recession is a perfect time for maintenance businesses. In a recession, people postpone purchasing new goods, while making their existing goods last longer.

If your company sells products, see if there isn't an opportunity to offer maintenance on those products. Or you might actually begin selling the used products (e.g. a distributor of industrial machines doubling as a used machine broker). Or, could you market refurbishing services? What about offering maintenance contracts? Spare parts? Think of ways to keep your customers from buying something new—it might lead to new business.

Seek cooperative efforts

As I've said before, the trick to marketing in a recession is to keep your name on the street without spending as much. Cooperative marketing efforts—that involve your company tying in with another—help you do just that. By bundling your products or services together with those of a complimentary company, you'll have increased your market exposure and developed another sales force of sorts. Efforts like these inevitably lead to new projects or sales and referrals you never would have been exposed to otherwise. Here are some joint promotional ideas that can accomplish both:

Joint Promotional Ideas

○ Launch a product or service that ties together your company's and another's service.

○ Link your marketing efforts together with the marketing efforts of another company (e.g. joint emails).

○ Swap databases with another company for direct mail efforts.

○ Make joint sales calls with another firm whose products are complimentary to yours.

○ Coordinate a co-op mailing where several other companies' materials are included.

Look to others for cooperative marketing efforts. They'll be doing the same and everyone can benefit if the fit is right.

Admit there's a recession

Jay Conrad Levinson, in his book *Guerilla Marketing Weapons*, says that being truthful is especially effective when marketing during a recession. People are overly concerned and suspicious, so you have to acknowledge these feelings—up front.

In your copy, recognize that there's a recession, and then target your products or services to "these troubled times." Honestly admit you *know* your audience is doubtful, then offer your service in the best light to help allay their fears.

How? Offer a trial period. Explain your guarantee. Clearly state what 800 numbers and customer support is available during your trial period. Whatever steps you need to take to address their fears, take them.

In the end, people want to hear the unvarnished truth. During a recession, let them know *you* know it's bad out there and it just might help you close that sale.

Publish a smile in all your marketing efforts

People are sad and scared during a recession; it's just human nature. That's why you'll stand out in people's minds if you stay upbeat. Do everything you can to be upbeat when talking with customers. Even if you're getting knocked around, answer "Outstanding" when someone asks how your day is going.

You'll be surprised at the infectious nature of your attitude, and people will feel better being around you. They'll want to talk to you more frequently because you *make them feel better*. And those warm feelings towards you and your business, will carry on long after the recession is over.

Plan for the long haul

The primary objective in a recession is survival—pure and simple. Many companies will falter—some will even close. But yours doesn't have to be one of them. By taking a long-term view of your business, with survival being your ultimate goal, you'll worry less about the day-to-day things.

Resolve to keep your marketing effort firing on all cylinders during the recession, albeit with a lower octane fuel. Keep your eyes on the prize—and you'll ride an upward curve once the economy pulls out of the recession.

Remember...

Recessions aren't a lot of fun, but they aren't the end of the world either. Plan for these stormy days, keep your marketing hat on and challenge yourself to be creative. Keep your frequency, cut costs and focus on your survival. When the smoke clears, you'll be surprised at the good fortune that comes your way!

Tools To Go

○ Although not a lot of fun, recessions are a great opportunity to make inroads with your marketing.

○ Keep the same frequency, but find ways to pare down costs.

○ Focus on more economical marketing campaigns such as phoning or email marketing.

○ Plan for the long haul—the average recession lasts 11 months.

Glossary

Advertising – any paid form of non-personal communication or presentation of a product, service, idea or company.

Advocate – a company's most loyal customers who usually provide very valuable word-of-mouth about the company and its products.

Affinity – an association or relationship (e.g. church membership) that indicates a similarity in lifestyle between individuals.

Appeal – the stated advantage of buying a product, as described in marketing communications for that product (e.g. advertising, promotions, publicity, sales literature).

Attributes – the features of a product that are thought to appeal to customers.

Audience – homes or individuals watching, reading, seeing or listening to a given media vehicle.

Awareness – movement of information about your product, service or company into a prospect's conscious mind. Often the desired objective of an advertising campaign and a principal goal of public relations.

Back-end – all marketing activities designed to convert inquiries into orders, as well as promotions directed at previous buyers.

Banner ad – the most common form of online advertising, banner ads come in a variety of standard sizes, and appear on a Web page as a box containing text, images, animation or other effects. Users who click on a banner follow a hyperlink to the advertiser's Web site.

Benefits – the satisfaction or fulfillment of needs that a customer receives from your products or services. In "My factories make cosmetics, we sell hope", hope is the benefit.

Billboard – popular name for outdoor advertising signage.

Body copy – the words in a marketing message that support and amplify the headline & subhead. The purpose of the body copy is to convince someone to buy your product.

Brand – the combination of symbols, words, or designs that differentiate one company's product from another's. Brand is also used to describe a company's family of products. A brand of coffee, for instance, might include its regular variety, as well as, its decaffeinated and instant varieties.

Brand awareness – the extent to which a brand or brand name is recognized by potential buyers.

Brand name – a protected, proprietary trademark of a manufacturer or products or services.

Break even analysis – the analysis of a product or service to determine the sales level required to cover both fixed costs of providing the product and the marketing & sales costs behind it.

Break even point – the specific sales level required to cover the fixed costs + marketing & sales costs of providing a product or service.

Brochure – a produced communication piece that's typically printed on heavier paper stock and features details about a company, its products or services.

Budget – the detailed financial component of a plan that guides the allocation of resources. It should also provide a means to measure deviation of actual vs. desired results for analysis.

Bundling – offering several complimentary products together or offering services, together with a product, in a single package deal. The price of the bundle is typically lower than the sum of the prices of the individual products or services included in it.

Business cycle – the movement of a business over time from birth through growth and maturity to decline. This is especially important these days as change comes about very quickly.

Business plan – a comprehensive written document that details a business's goals and the marketing, operational and organizational directions it will take to achieve these goals over the next 3-5 years.

Business-to-business – advertising or promotion intended to influence corporate awareness and purchase.

Call-to-action – a highly motivating statement that tells the reader what action they should take next and exactly how to do it (example: "Call 1-800-555-1213 now to order").

Campaign – a coordinated advertising and promotion effort intended to continue thematically over time.

Capabilities brochure – promotional brochure stating what your company does and the general capabilities you offer customers. It can include general information as well as very specific details about the company and its operations.

Channel – a group of retailers or distributors through whom a product is distributed. A company may have several channels, each of which is used to reach different end-users or categories of customers.

Channel marketing – a way of organizing marketing functions in a company that puts individuals in charge of selling to specific classes of trade.

Click-through – The process of clicking on a link in a search engine output page to visit an indexed site.

Collateral – any and all printed materials designed to support a brand or company's promotional effort.

Competition – businesses competing for the same market dollars.

Consumer – the person who actually uses the product or service. Also called a 'customer', 'patron', 'buyer' , 'shopper' or 'end user'.

Contingency plan – an acceptable alternative plan that can be implemented in the event a basic plan is aborted or changed for any reason.

Co-operative advertising – an arrangement whereby a product or service is brought to the public's attention using the names of the supplier and the intermediary (e.g. a cereal manufacturer and a grocery retailer jointly promoting a cereal).

Copywriting – writing text for an ad or promotional piece.

CPI – cost per inquiry. Arrived at by dividing the total marketing costs by the number of inquiries (example: $2,500 marketing costs/25 inquiries=$100 CPI).

CPO – cost per order. Arrived at by dividing the total marketing costs by the number of orders (example: $2,500 marketing costs/5 orders=$500 CPO).

Creative – general description of the activity related to the development of promotional materials. Includes concepts, design, and copy.

Customer – loosely, any buyer of a product or service, at any trade level. Also called a consumer or patron.

Customer feedback – compliments, criticisms, or general information provided to a company by its customers about products, services or other aspects of the business.

Customer Relationship Management (CRM) – a business strategy to select and manage customers to optimize long-term value.

Database Marketing – the use of information that's been electronically stored and analyzed about prospects or customer behaviors. This information is then used to determine appropriate marketing activities in order to influence purchases and future sales.

Deadline – a concrete time limit. Can be used for projects, subprojects, offers and a variety of other marketing uses.

Demographics – statistics about the socioeconomic makeup of a population including age, gender, race, occupation, income, education.

Differentiation – establishing a distinction in the mind of a customer about products, services or a company.

Direct mail – marketing materials sent directly to a prospect or customer via the U.S. Postal Service or a private delivery company.

Directory – websites with look-up capabilities that assign other websites to categories. Directories are edited by humans, as opposed to search engines, which are edited by spiders.

Discount – a reduction in the stated rate or list price, usually offered in the form of a percentage and used as an incentive to make a purchase.

Distribution – the delivery or conveyance of a good/service to a market.

Distribution channel – the chain or intermediaries linking the producer of a good to the consumer.

Distributor – a firm or individual, particularly a wholesaler, who sells or delivers merchandise to customers (i.e. retail stores).

Domain name – the text-based URL or address of a Web site. Domain names usually consist of several different segments. The name www.emergemarketing.com, for example, includes the generic "www." and ".com" identifiers, along with the unique name "emergemarketing."

Exit interview – an interview conducted at the end of an employee's term of employment to obtain honest employment feedback.

External analysis – analysis of those factors outside your business, which present opportunities or threats.

FAQ (frequently asked questions) – a listing of common questions and answers related to a company, product or Web site, FAQs can help users get answers without overburdening human support staff and can be used strategically to attract traffic to a web site.

Feature – a characteristic or property of a product/service such as reliability, price, convenience, safety, quality, size.

Flyer – an inexpensive, 1-page promotional sheet (usually $8^{1}/_{2}$ x 11") typically intended for handout or bulk mailing.

Frequency – how many times a person buys from you, how many times a marketing message is exposed to a target audience or how many times a program is run.

Front-end – all marketing activities designed to generate inquiries. *See back end*

Gantt Chart – a planning tool and the basis for marketing timelines in this book. In simple terms, a timeline showing the various timing among events.

Gatekeeper – someone within an organization who doesn't directly consume a product or service but does control access to decision makers and thus, wields considerable influence in the purchase process.

Goals – objectives for a marketing effort to achieve. "Dreams with a deadline".

Hard Goals – a goal that can be quantified and measured.

Headline – a sentence, phrase or words that appear above a body of text. The purpose of a headline is to attract attention and prod the reader to continue reading.

Hit – a hit is the result of a file being requested and served from your web site. This can be an html document, an image file, an audio track, etc. Web pages that contain a large number of elements will return high hit scores. Thus, hits are of very little consequence when analyzing your visitor demographics.

Home page – the main (or first) page of a website.

House List – a list of names already owned by a company consisting of purchasers or buyer inquiries and used by the company to promote its products & services.

Hyperlink (or link) – web developers use HTML to create hyperlinks that a user clicks on to view another Web page. Hyperlinks can appear as graphics or as areas of differently colored or underlined text.

Image – the way a company or organization is perceived by the public and its customers.

Impressions – the total number of exposures provided by a particular medium.

Inserts – extra printed pages inserted loosely into printed pieces. Inserts are often advertising supplements to a newspaper or magazine.

Integrated marketing communications – coordination across a variety of promotional vehicles that ensures all marketing messages are clear and consistent. The outcome of integrated communications is synergy.

Internal analysis – analysis of the internal strengths & weaknesses of your company.

Internet – a network of networks, built upon a set of widely used software protocols that link millions of computers around the world. Services such as email and the Web use the Internet to transfer data.

JPEG (Joint Photographic Experts Group) – one of the two most common image types used on the Web (GIF is the other). JPEG is used mostly for photographic reproductions. Also referred to as jpg.

Keywords – descriptive words that are embedded in your website code. Common places to use keywords are in your web pages, for search engine registration, and for directory listings

Leapfrogging – a strategy aimed at overtaking your competition and creating the future shape of the industry.

Lead – a new and unqualified prospect or client, previously unknown to a sales person or company. Also called an inquiry.

Lead generation – marketing tactics used to solicit leads for sales follow up and including direct mailings, tradeshows, networking and others.

Leave-behind – documents or premiums that a salesperson leaves with prospects or customers to remind them of the product or service.

Lifetime value – the total profit or loss estimated or realized from a customer over the active life of that customer.

Link – a function that takes a user, with just one click, from one page on the web to another.

List broker – a person or company who prepares, rents and maintains mailing lists.

List price – the price regularly quoted to customers before applying discounts. These are usually the prices printed on dealer lists, invoices, price tags, catalogs or dealer purchase orders.

List segmentation – the use of subgroups within a list usually sharing similar demographic, target niche or buying characteristics.

Logo – a distinctive company symbol that helps create an image or brand.

Mailing list – a list of customers or prospects used to mail catalogs or sales announcements. It is not a marketing database because it does not provide for a two-way communication with customers.

Market penetration – the percentage of buyers you have as compared with the total households or businesses in the area you've selected as your market.

Market research – data pertaining to customers within a market segment.

Market segment – a group of actual or potential customers who can be expected to respond in approximately the same way to a given offer.

Market segmentation – the act of dividing up a market into distinct groups of buyers so as to better target your marketing efforts.

Market share – the % of total buyers for a product or service who choose to buy from your company.

Marketing audit (or assessment) – an analysis of the company's current marketplace, current marketing capabilities and potential opportunities.

Marketing consultant – an individual or firm who by training and experience is qualified to help a company with its marketing efforts.

Marketing integration – the coordination of all marketing strategies so they work together to establish a maximum impact in the market.

Marketing mix – the combination of all elements used to market a product or service. These include product, price, place (distribution) and promotion.

Marketing plan – the annual planning document that sets the marketing direction for a product, service or company. It spells out the strategies, tactics, timelines and budgetary details for accomplishing the marketing objectives.

Marketing strategy(ies) – the broad directional thrusts a business uses to achieve its marketing goals. Characterized by broad decisions concerning price, product, distribution and/or promotional issues.

Marketing tactics – the executable elements or actual steps the marketers will take to achieve the objectives and strategies.

Mass marketing – a marketing strategy in which a seller develops one product offering for all buyers in the market.

Medium (pl. media) – a type of publication or communications method that conveys news, entertainment and advertising to an audience. Examples include newspapers, television, magazines, radio, billboards and the Internet.

Meta Tags – hidden descriptions of your web pages that describe the page's content and help attract the attention of search engines.

Metrics – the measurements a marketer uses to analyze and assess a marketing effort.

Mission Statement – a formal statement of the reason your company or organization exists. It may include a series of goals or objectives that the organization wishes to achieve.

Mnemonic device – any device designed to enhance the recognition or memorability of a brand.

Multimedia – information that combines different types of content, such as text, images, animation, video and audio.

Niche marketing – a way of finding a special product that appeals to only one group, and selling that product very profitably only to that group.

Objectives – medium-term goals which are specific, measurable and realistic.

OEM (original equipment manufacturer) – a company that produces equipment bearing another company's label.

Offer – what you offer, as an inducement to buy, in your direct mail (e.g. buy one, get one free).

Opt-in vehicles – any marketing vehicle (but usually Internet-based vehicles) that allow all recipients to first agree to receive the vehicle. With opt-in vehicles, the recipient tells you it's okay to send him or her future editions of the vehicle. These vehicles generally generate better response because the recipients have indicated an interest from the outset.

Order(s) – the point where a customer agrees to exchange money for goods or services provided by a company. Can also be called a purchase order.

Page view – a page view is registered each time a page from your website is loaded or reloaded onto someone's browser. It is not a good indicator of how many different people are visiting your web site. Yet, it can be a good way to judge the "stickiness" (ability to retain visitors' interest) of your site.

Patent – an exclusive ownership interest in an invention for a designated period of years, granted by the government.

Personal sales – the sales tactic where direct contact between the customer and the company representative takes place for the purpose of gaining a sale.

Personalization – the means of adding personal information such as the individual's name to a mailing piece.

Planning – the process of pre-determining a course or courses of action based on assumptions about future conditions or trends.

Position – the perception that a marketer attempts to convey about a brand and its benefits vis-à-vis the competition.

Positioning – a marketing strategy that attempts to positively influence the perception of a company, product or service relative to its competitors & competitive products & services.

Pre-test – the testing of a research survey (or, for that matter, any marketing program) before launching it in order to fine tune the survey administration.

Press kit – a collection of publicity materials, including press releases and general company information, that is packaged and sent to media outlets.

Press release – a document that communicates information to the press. Press releases can publicize good news such as positive earnings and new product launches, or they can help control the damage caused by bad news.

Price – the amount of money asked for in the transfer of products and services from the provider(s) to the consumer(s).

Pricing strategy – pricing for long-term advantage rather than short-term profits.

Product – a manufactured good that possesses objective and subjective characteristics that are manipulated to maximize the item's appeal to customers.

Product life cycle – the pattern of growth and decline in sales revenue of a product over time.

Promotion – all forms of communication other than advertising that call attention to products and services, typically by adding extra value to the purchase. Includes temporary discounts, allowances, premium offers, coupons, contests and rebates.

Prospect – identified consumers, be they individuals or companies, who show good potential for buying a company's products or services and have made contact with a company. *See suspects.*

Psychographics – shared attitudes or behaviors of population groups.

Public domain information – the tremendous wealth of information that is open and available to anyone who seeks it.

Public relations – communication with various sectors of the public—including media relations, employee relations and community relations—and designed to influence their attitudes and opinions in the interest of promoting a person, product or idea.

Publicity – information with news value used to promote a product, service or idea in the media.

Rationale – a logical reasoning for choosing a strategy.

Reach – the total number of individuals or companies that are exposed to a marketing vehicle.

Recency – a term for how recent a person has purchased from your company. It is well established that people who have purchased most recently are more likely to buy from you again on your next promotion.

Referral – name of a prospective customer that was acquired from a current customer or other third party.

Relationship marketing – understanding the customer so well that their needs are met to a consistent standard of excellence which turns customers into very loyal customers.

Sales forecast – educated guesstimates of future revenues segmented into individual SBU's or product sales.

Sales incentive – a reward, usually in the form of cash or product, for members of the sales staff who achieve a specific goal or an annual quota.

Sales Message – the ideas, concepts and points a company conveys via various selling methods.

Sales plan – the definable steps a company takes to secure sales.

Search engine – online software that helps users locate information and other sites on the Internet.

Search engine – an online database that enables Internet users to locate other websites, containing information they need. Every search engine has its own strategy for collecting data so, one search usually turns up different results on different search engines.

Seasonality – the variations in sales or response that are attributable to the change in season. For example, hot cocoa's seasonality is stronger in winter, while iced tea mix is stronger in the summer.

Segment – a portion of a list or file selected on the basis of a special set of characteristics.

Self-mailer – A direct mail piece, such as a postcard or tabbed newsletter, which does not require an envelope or wrapper for mailing.

Service – any activity provided by a person or company to another person or company that is intangible. Services can be provided separate from products or they can be bundled together with a product.

Spam – slang term for unsolicited commercial email. "Spamming" people with unwanted commercial email solicitations is considered unethical and is now illegal in several U.S. states. Most internet service providers (ISP's) will terminate a user's account if it's used to send spam.

Spiders – a search engine's automated program that indexes web documents, titles and/or a portion of each document. These documents are acquired by the spider as it automatically traverses across the Internet (kinda scary, huh?).

Strategic alliance – the sharing of information, methods, marketing and finance between complimentary businesses.

Strategic Business Unit (SBU) – a company division, product line or single brand that can be marketed independently from the rest of the company.

Strength – an asset, capability or intangible of a company that potentially provides it with a competitive advantage.

Suspects – identified consumers, be they individuals or companies, who show good potential for buying a company's products or services but have not yet made contact with a company. *See prospect.*

Tactics – the actual programs and techniques used to accomplish a strategy.

Target market – the defined group of consumers that a marketer considers to be prime prospects (i.e. most likely to purchase).

Target marketing – where different products, pricing, distribution methods and promotions are developed to meet consumers varying needs and preferences.

Task – an individual unit of work that is part of the total work needed to accomplish a project.

Telemarketing – using the telephone to sell, promote or solicit products and services.

Test market – trial market for a new product, service, offer or other marketing effort.

Timeline – a specific action plan, laid out in a visual format, that lines out the various tactics the company will pursue and the subsequent deadlines.

Touchpoint – any place where a business comes into contact with its customers or prospects. Generally considered to be personal contact points (e.g. trade shows, phone calls) as opposed to non-personal ones (e.g. brochures, websites, advertisements).

Trademark – the name, phrase, logo, image or combination of images of a product/brand claimed as owned by a marketer. The term is often used to include service marks, which apply to businesses providing services as opposed to selling products.

Trial – the initial customer use of a product/service. Either given away free or sold at a nominal price, to gain customer experience with the brand.

Trial offer – the offer to a consumer to try a product for a stated period of time before deciding whether or not to purchase.

Two-step – in direct mail, a selling process that first solicits a request for information (inquiry) then, as a second step, follows up with additional mailings to close the sale.

Unique selling proposition – the key, unique benefit that differentiates your product/service from all your competitors. Made famous by Rosser Reeves, an ad giant of the 1950's.

Unique visitor – someone with a unique IP address (when you log onto the Internet, you are assigned a unique IP address) who enters a Web site for the first time, during a set period of time. Different traffic monitoring programs define this period differently, however you'll find most defining it between 2 hours and 24 hours. This measure is, by far, the most accurate way of analyzing web site performance.

Upsell – A technique to increase the value or quantity of a sale by suggesting additional options or upgrades. For example, a fast-food restaurant may upsell by suggesting that a customer buy a larger portion of a drink.

URL – Universal Resource Locator. The text address that allows users to find a particular Web site or Web page (www.emergemarketing.com).

Value-added – any promotional, product or service technique that seeks to add value to the product.

Value-added reseller – a dealer, say in the high tech industry, who specializes in "solution sales" which combine consulting, needs analysis and bundling of turnkey packages.

Vision Statement – a vivid description of where your company or strategic business unit (SBU) wants to be after a period of time—say 5 years.

Web browser – a program that allows an individual to view Web pages.

Web host – a service that operates Web servers for its clients and publishes their Web sites.

Web page – a page in a Web document. Unlike printed pages, a Web page may be just a few words long or it may include thousands of words, images and other content.

Web server – a computer that publishes a Web site on the Internet. It usually includes the Web server software, the appropriate software protocols such as TCP/IP, the Web site content and occasionally other software such as e-commerce or database applications.

Weakness – a shortcoming of a company that potentially could place it at a competitive disadvantage.

Wholesaler – a business that buys goods from manufacturers, then sells the goods, usually in larger quantities, to retailers, who in turn, sell them to the end user. A middleman between the manufacturer and the retailer.

Word-of-mouth advertising (or just word-of-mouth) – getting satisfied customers to recommend the product or service to friends, family, co-workers or anyone else they're familiar with. This kind of advertising costs the provider nothing and very often is viewed as more credible than information provided directly by the manufacturer.

World Wide Web (or the Web) – an Internet service that links collections of documents, or Web sites, both internally and to other sites. In addition to formatted text, Web pages may include graphics, audio, video and other Multimedia content.

Recommended Resources

Books

Bangs, David: *The Market Planning Guide,* Upstart Publishing, IL, 1995

Barrett, Fred: *Names That Sell: How to Create Great Names for Your Company, Product or Service,* Alder Press, OR, 1995

Bayan, Richard: *Words that Sell,* Contemporary Books, IL, 1984

Bacon, Mark S.: *Do-it-Yourself Direct Marketing,* John Wiley & Sons, Inc., 1997

Beckwith, Harry: *Selling the Invisible: A Field Guide to Modern Marketing,* Warner Books, NY, 1997

Burroughs Blake, George & Nancy Blake-Bohne: *Crafting the Perfect Name,* Probus Publishing Company, IL, 1991

Blankenship, A.B., et al: *State of the Art Marketing Research,* NTC Business Books, 1998

Bly, Robert: *Selling Your Services,* Henry Holt & Company, NY, 1991

Breen, George Edward & Dutka, Alan: *State of the Art Marketing Research,* NTC Business Books, IL, 1998

Breen, George Edward & Blankenship, A.B.: *Do-it-Yourself Marketing Research,* McGraw-Hill, NY, 1989

Bristol, Claude: *The Magic of Believing,* Simon & Schuster, NY, 1948

Caples, John: *Tested Advertising Methods,* Prentice-Hall, NJ, 1974

Cook, Kenneth J.: *AMA Complete Guide to Small Business Marketing,* NTC Business Books, IL, 1993

Crainer, Stuart: *The Ultimate Business Library; 50 Books That Shaped Management,* AMACOM, NY, 1997

Evans, Fred J., *Managing the Media,* Quorum Books, New York, NY 1987

Floyd, Elaine, *Marketing With Newsletters*, Newsletter Resources, St. Louis, MO 1997

Forest, Edward, *Interactive Marketing; The Future Present*, NTC Books, Chicago, IL 1996

Friedman, Jack P., *Dictionary of Business Terms,* Barrons Educational Service 1987

Godin, Seth, *Permission Marketing,* Simon & Schuster, NY 1990

Godin, Seth, *Unleashing the Idea Virus*, Do You Zoom, Inc. NY 2000

Gray, Daniel, *Looking Good on the Web*, The Coriolis Group, AZ 1999

Hall, Robert E., *The Streetcorner Strategy for Winning Local Markets,* 1993

Harding, Ford, *Rain Making: The Professional's Guide to Attracting New Clients*, Bob Adams, Inc, MA 1994

Hiam, Alexander, *Marketing for Dummies*, IDG Books 1997

Hunt, John F., *The Do-it-Yourself Marketing Handbook*, Better Books, LLC, IA 1998

Kahaner, Larry, *Competitive Intelligence*, Simon & Schuster, New York, NY 1996

Kennedy, Daniel, *The Ultimate Marketing Plan*, Bob Adams, Inc, MA 1991

Kobs, Jim, *Profitable Direct Marketing*, NTC Business Books, IL 1993

Lambert, Tom, *High Income Consulting*, Nicholas Brealey Publishing, London 1993

Levine, Rick et al, *The Cluetrain Manifesto*, Perseus Books, MA 2000

Levinson, Jay & Seth Godin, *The Guerilla Marketing Handbook*, Houghton Mifflin, MA 1994

Levinson, Jay Conrad, *Guerilla Marketing Weapons*, 1990

Levinson, Jay Conrad, *Mastering Guerilla Marketing; 100 Profit-Producing Insights You Can Take to the Bank*, Houghton Mifflin, Inc., MA 1999

McDonald, Malcolm, *Marketing By Matrix,* NTC Business Books, IL 1993

Nagel, Thomas and Holden, Reed, *The Strategy and Tactics of Pricing,* Prentice Hall, NJ 1995

Ogden, James R., *Developing a Creative and Innovative Integrated Marketing Communications Plan; A Working Model,* Prentice Hall, NJ 1990

Ortman, Mark, *Now That Makes Sense; Relating To People With Wit and Wisdom,* Wise Owl Books, WA 1993

Porter, Michael, *Competitive Advantage,* The Free Press, NY 1985

Porter, Michael, *Competitive Strategy,* The Free Press, NY 1980

Ries, Al and Jack Trout, *Positioning: The Battle for Your Mind,* Warner Books, NY 1986

Ries, Al and Jack Trout, *The 22 Immutable Laws of Marketing,* 1994

Rolnicki, Kenneth, *Managing Channels of Distribution,* AMACOM, New York, NY 1998

Saffir, Leonard, *Power Public Relations,* NTC Business Books, Chicago, IL 2000

Schmitt, Bernd, *Marketing Aesthetics; The Strategic Management of Brands,* The Free Press, New York, NY 1997

Seybold, Patricia, *The Customer Revolution,* Crown Business, NY 2001

Wechsler, Warren, *The 6 Steps to Excellence in Selling,* Better Books, LLC Fairfield, IA 1995

Weinstein, Art, *Market Segmentation,* Probus Publishing, Chicago, IL 1994

Young, Davis, *Building Your Company's Good Name,* AMACON, New York, NY, 1996

Yovovich, B.G., *New Marketing Imperatives,* Prentice-Hall, NJ 1995

Yudkin, Marsha, *6 Steps to Free Publicity,* Penguin Books, NY 1994

Websites for Marketers

www.yudkin.com
Marcia Yudkin is an accomplished author and puts out a relevant and pithy weekly newsletter called The Marketing Minute.

www.emergemarketing.com
I'd be remiss if I didn't mention our company's website. There you'll find tips, tools and free downloads to help marketers at all levels. Free e-newsletter.

www.nua.ie/surveys
Touting itself as "the world's leading resource for Internet trends and statistics", this site does offer a wide variety of current data on web trends.

www.ientry.com
iEntry, Inc. publishes a wide variety of electronic newsletters.

www.completeresults.com
A weekly Internet promotion ezine. Their free newsletter is really quite good. Covers topics as varied as autoresponders, search engines, web tactics

www.DrNunley.com
A pretty good site for marketing writing tips. Free newsletter.

www.clickz.com

www.websitesecrets.com

www.websecrets.com

Index

Sample Marketing Plan
XYZ Company

1. Mission Statement

XYZ Corporation's Lead Division mission statement is:

"Our mission is to provide quality products and services through environmentally safe recycling"

2. Quantitative Goals

The company' s quantitative goals are:

What	How Much	By when	Whom
Increase lead sold	to 95K Tons	by 12/31/01	Marketing & Sales Team
Keep profitability	between $20-50 per ton	thru 12/31/01	Marketing & Sales Team
Get 15K tons	from never-before ordered customers	by 12/31/01	Marketing & Sales Team

3. Qualitative Goals

The company's qualitative goals are:

What	By when	So that...	Whom
Tighten our positioning & focus by 12/31/01, so that we stand out from our competitors—Marketing & Sales Team			
Improve the way we communicate our capabilities by 12/31/01, so that it's clear what XYZ does—and doesn't do—Marketing & Sales Team			

4. Key Problems

In establishing its marketing and sales problems, the team first identified all known problems. Then each problem was prioritized. Those highest-ranking problems are shaded and incorporated into the plan.

Marketing Problems:		
	Type	Priority
• No marketing plan	(Process)	3
• Need greater frequency in customer contact	(Promotion)	2.75
• Current point-of-difference carries less weight w/market	(Promotion)	1.75
• Capabilities piece could use a "brush-up"	(Promotion)	1.5
• Limited geographic market with current operation	(Place)	1.5

5. Current Products & Services

The market for lead alloys is a commodity market. There is little product differentiation among suppliers and the market is marked by acquisition and consolidations. Price is a dominant purchase motivator.

There are ways for producers to differentiate themselves in a commodity market. One way for XYZ to distinguish itself from the competition is through value-added services to its existing customer base. By offering services to strengthen ties with customers, it can distinguish itself from competitors.

6. Target Audiences

There are three target audience groups for the Company. All marketing efforts will be concentrated on reaching and influencing them.

#1 Customers

Industries:
Automotive batteries & parts
Industrial batteries
Ammunition
Sporting goods equipment

Purchasing Individual:
Gender: 95% Male
Department: Purchasing Dept.
Operations & Exec. staff

Location: w/in 600 Mile Radius

Without a continuous raw material supply (used car batteries), XYZ suffers out-of-stocks and fails to deliver on one of its perceived strengths—available supplies.

So, a primary focus of the marketing effort will be to market and raise XYZ's awareness among upstream dealers.

#3 Community Groups XYZ's marketing efforts must seek to indirectly appeal to several community groups. These include:

Neighbors/Residents/Employees
Political bodies
Regulatory agencies

Meetings and informal discussions with community members are, and will continue to be, the primary communication method for this audience. However, if positive actions occur from the marketing plan (e.g. publicity, events) and it makes sense to involve the community members, XYZ will do this.

7. Competitors

3 of your customers, interviewed by Emerge Marketing, identified these strengths and weaknesses in XYZ's competitors:

Competitor	Strengths	Weaknesses
Hexide	*Location*—more national locations	*Pricing*
RJR	*Price*—very competitive pricing	*Distance*
Deer Run	*Product*—superior product quality	*Distance & Pricing*
	Promote—heavily advertise & promote	

8. Positioning Worksheet

Drawing on the previous information, and XYZ's extensive experience in the market, the marketing & sales team came up with the following information about XYZ's positioning.

Key Advantages

What really sets us apart from the competition?

1. We're faster, more nimble
2. We're honest
3. We're accessible

Competitive Weaknesses

What's wrong with competing products/service providers?

1. They're elephants (they're big & slow-moving)
2. They're snakes (they're not honest, they're under-the-table)

Unique Selling Proposition

What single message about our product OR company is most likely to generate a positive buying response?

• XYZ—a lead smelter you could bring home to your mother (honesty)

9. Marketing Strategies & Tactics

STRATEGY: *Develop online, value-added services to support "Customer Intimate" model*

RATIONALE: *Service can be differentiating factor for XYZ*

TACTICS: *Put up online inventory, ordering, order tracking, purchase history*

Tactics	Complete Date	Task Lead
Develop team	Done	Dan, John
Write cost estimate	Done	Dan, Team
Make go/no go decision	Jul 15	Dan, Team
Roll-out online system	Dec 15	Team

STRATEGY: *Continue sales & networking efforts*
RATIONALE: *Helps prioritize activities in industry dependent on face-to-face networking; will help uncover new business opportunities*

Tactics	Complete Date	Task Lead
Account planning mtg w/Jay, Dan, John, Mark	Done	Team
Rough out plan, by account; large & small account objectives, action steps	Done	Jay
Present to Team	Jun 25	Jay, Team

STRATEGY: *Pursue packaging improvements*
RATIONALE: *Helps create awareness of XYZ product among customer's operations staff*

Tactics	Complete Date	Task Lead
Assign Taskforce	Jul 1	John
Develop project description	TBD	John, taskforce
Finalize recommendations/ costing	End Aug	John, taskforce
Test new packaging	Dec.	John, taskforce

STRATEGY: *Refine positioning & incorporate into materials*
RATIONALE: *Need to update primary selling messages due to market's catching up on quality standards*

Tactics	Complete Date	Task Lead
Present next steps & cost estimate to team (positioning work, collateral refresh)	Jun 25	Jay
Schedule positioning session	Jul	Jay

* *Timelines and Budgets would be separate attachments*

Order Form

Please send me _____ copy (copies) of **_The Marketing Toolkit for Growing Businesses,_ by Jay Lipe,** at a cost of $23.95 each (includes a $4.00 shipping and handling cost).

Sales Tax: Please add 6.5% for products shipped to Minnesota addresses.

For International Orders: All International orders will be in USD$. Shipping international is $9 USD for first book, $2 USD for each additional book.

○ **Check enclosed for $_____(USD$)**

○ **Bill my credit card (Visa or Mastercard)**

Card number: _____

Expiration date: _____

Name on card:_____

Name: _____

Address: _____

City: _____ State: _____ Zip: _____

Telephone: _____

Email address: _____

○ **Yes, I would like the book(s) autographed to:_____**

_____

**Please send me
FREE information on:**

○ Speaking/Seminars

○ Consulting

Mail or fax to:

Chammerson Press

4315 Aldrich Ave. S.
Minneapolis, MN 55409-1810

Phone: (612) 824-2198
Fax: (612) 824-8597

Order Form

Please send me _____ copy (copies) of **The Marketing Toolkit for Growing Businesses, by Jay Lipe,** at a cost of $23.95 each (includes a $4.00 shipping and handling cost).

Sales Tax: Please add 6.5% for products shipped to Minnesota addresses.

For International Orders: All International orders will be in USD$. Shipping international is $9 USD for first book, $2 USD for each additional book.

○ **Check enclosed for $_____(USD$)**

○ **Bill my credit card (Visa or Mastercard)**

Card number: _____

Expiration date: _____

Name on card:_____

Name: _____

Address: _____

City: _____ State: _____ Zip: _____

Telephone: _____

Email address: _____

○ **Yes, I would like the book(s) autographed to:_____**

_____

Please send me FREE information on:

○ Speaking/Seminars

○ Consulting

Mail or fax to:

Chammerson Press

4315 Aldrich Ave. S.
Minneapolis, MN 55409-1810

Phone: (612) 824-2198
Fax: (612) 824-8597